दुर्गा

দুর্গা পূজা

Durgā Pūjā

BEGINNER

by

Swami Satyananda Saraswati

दुर्गा पूजा দুর্গা পূজা **Durgā Pūjā**

by Devi Mandir Publications
5950 Highway 128
Napa, CA 94558 USA
Communications: Phone and Fax 1-707-966-2802
E-Mail swamiji@shreemaa.org
Please visit us on the World Wide Web at
http://www.shreemaa.org

ISBN 1-877795-30-5
Library of Congress Catalog Card Number
CIP 2001 126530

दुर्गा पूजा দুর্গা পূজা **Durgā Pūjā**
Swami Satyananda Saraswati
1. Hindu Religion. 2. Worship. 3. Spirituality.
4. Philosophy. I. Saraswati, Swami Satyananda;

ॐ कात्यायनाय विद्महे कन्याकुमारी धीमहि ।

तन्नो दुर्गिः प्रचोदयात् ॐ ॥

ওঁ কাত্যায়নায় বিদ্মহে কন্যাকুমারী

ধীমহি । তন্নো দুর্গিঃ প্রচোদয়াত্ ওঁ ।।

oṃ kātyāyanāya vidmahe kanyākumārī dhīmahi
tanno durgiḥ pracodayāt oṃ

oṃ We meditate upon the Ever Pure One, contemplate the Daughter Without Flaw or Imperfection. May that Goddess grant us increase.

(Wave light)

ॐ अग्नि ज्योति रवि ज्योतिष्चन्द्र ज्योतिष्तथैव च ।

ज्योतिशमुत्तमो देवी दीपोऽयं प्रतिगृह्यतम् ॥

एष दीपः ॐ ह्रीं श्रीं दुं दुर्गायै नमः

ওঁ অগ্নি জ্যোতি রবি জ্যোতিষ্চন্দ্র জ্যোতিষ্তথৈব চ ।

জ্যোতিশমুত্তমো দেবী দীপোহয়ং প্রতিগৃহ্যতম্ ।।

এষ দীপঃ ওঁ হ্রীং শ্রীং দুং দুর্গায়ৈ নমঃ

oṃ agni jyoti ravi jyotiṣ candra jyotiṣ tathaiva ca
jyoti śamuttamo devī dīpo-yaṃ pratigṛhyatam
eṣa dīpaḥ oṃ hrīṃ śrīṃ duṃ durgāyai namaḥ

oṃ The Divine Fire is the Light, the Light of Wisdom is the Light, the Light of Devotion is the Light as well. The Light of the Highest Bliss, Oh Goddess, is in the Light which I offer, the Light which I request you to accept. We bow to the Goddess, Durgā, the Grantor of Increase, who Removes all Difficulties.

ave incense)

ॐ वनस्पतिरसोत्पन्नो गन्ध्यात्येया गन्ध्य उत्तमः ।

आघ्रेयः सर्व देवानां धूपोऽयं प्रतिगृह्यतम् ॥

एष धूपः ॐ ह्रीं श्रीं दुं दुर्गायै नमः

ওঁ বনস্পতিরসোত্পন্নো গন্ধ্যাত্যেয়া গন্ধ্য উত্তমঃ ।

আঘ্রেয়ঃ সর্ব দেবানাং ধূপোঽয়ং প্রতিগৃহ্যতম্ ।।

এষ ধূপঃ ওঁ হ্রীং শ্রীং দুং দুর্গায়ৈ নমঃ

oṃ vanaspatirasotpanno gandhyātyeyā gandhya uttamaḥ
āghreyaḥ sarva devānāṃ dhūpo-yaṃ pratigṛhyatam
eṣa dhūpaḥ oṃ hrīṃ śrīṃ duṃ durgāyai namaḥ

oṃ Spirit of the Forest, from you is produced the most excellent of scents. The scent most pleasing to all the Gods, that scent I request you to accept. With the offering of fragrant scent oṃ We bow to the Goddess, Durgā, the Grantor of Increase, who Removes all Difficulties.

(Folded hands)

ॐ भूर्भुवः स्वः । तत् सवितुर्वरेण्यम् भर्गो देवस्य धीमहि ।

धियो यो नः प्रचोदयात् ॥

ওঁ ভূর্ভুবঃ স্বঃ । তৎ সবিতুর্বরেণ্যম্ ভর্গো দেবস্য

ধীমহি । ধিয়ো য়ো নঃ প্রচোদয়াৎ ।।

oṃ bhūr bhuvaḥ svaḥ
tat savitur vareṇyam bhargo devasya dhīmahi
dhiyo yo naḥ pracodayāt

Oṃ the Infinite Beyond Conception, the gross body, the subtle body and the causal body; we meditate upon that Light of Wisdom which is the Supreme Wealth of the Gods. May it grant to us increase in our meditations.

दुर्गा पूजा Durgā Pūjā

Offer a flower with each mantra ete gandhapuṣpe

एते गन्धपुष्पे ॐ गं गणपतये नमः

এতে গন্ধপুষ্পে ওঁ গং গণপতয়ে নমঃ

ete gandhapuṣpe oṃ gaṃ gaṇapataye namaḥ

With these scented flowers oṃ I bow to the Lord of Wisdom, Lord of the Multitudes.

एते गन्धपुष्पे ॐ अदित्यादि नवग्रहेभ्यो नमः

এতে গন্ধপুষ্পে ওঁ আদিত্যাদি নবগ্রহেভ্যো নমঃ

ete gandhapuṣpe oṃ ādityādi navagrahebhyo namaḥ

With these scented flowers oṃ I bow to the Sun, the Light of Wisdom, along with the nine planets.

एते गन्धपुष्पे ॐ शिवादिपञ्चदेवताभ्यो नमः

এতে গন্ধপুষ্পে ওঁ শিবাদিপঞ্চদেবতাভ্যো নমঃ

ete gandhapuṣpe oṃ śivādipañcadevatābhyo namaḥ

With these scented flowers oṃ I bow to Śiva, the Consciousness of Infinite Goodness, along with the five primary deities (Śiva, Śakti, Viṣṇu, Gaṇeṣa, Sūrya).

एते गन्धपुष्पे ॐ इन्द्रादिदशदिक्पालेभ्यो नमः

এতে গন্ধপুষ্পে ওঁ ইন্দ্রাদিদশদিক্পালেভ্যো নমঃ

ete gandhapuṣpe oṃ indrādi daśa dikpālebhyo namaḥ

With these scented flowers oṃ I bow to Indra, the Ruler of the Pure, along with the Ten Protectors of the ten diretions.

एते गन्धपुष्पे ॐ मत्स्यादिदशावतारेभ्यो नमः

এতে গন্ধপুষ্পে ওঁ মৎস্যাদিদশাবতারেভ্যো নমঃ

ete gandhapuṣpe oṃ matsyādi daśāvatārebhyo namaḥ

With these scented flowers oṃ I bow to Vishnu, the Fish, along with the Ten Incarnations which He assumed.

एते गन्धपुष्पे ॐ प्रजापतये नमः

এতে গন্ধপুষ্পে ওঁ প্রজাপতয়ে নমঃ

ete gandhapuṣpe oṃ prajāpataye namaḥ

With these scented flowers oṃ I bow to the Lord of All Created Beings.

एते गन्धपुष्पे ॐ नमो नारायणाय नमः

এতে গন্ধপুষ্পে ওঁ নমো নারায়ণায় নমঃ

ete gandhapuṣpe oṃ namo nārāyaṇāya namaḥ

With these scented flowers oṃ I bow to the Perfect Perception of Consciousness.

एते गन्धपुष्पे ॐ सर्वेभ्यो देवेभ्यो नमः

এতে গন্ধপুষ্পে ওঁ সর্বেভ্যো দেবেভ্যো নমঃ

ete gandhapuṣpe oṃ sarvebhyo devebhyo namaḥ

With these scented flowers oṃ I bow to All the Gods.

एते गन्धपुष्पे ॐ सर्वाभ्यो देवीभ्यो नमः

এতে গন্ধপুষ্পে ওঁ সর্বাভ্যো দেবীভ্যো নমঃ

ete gandhapuṣpe oṃ sarvābhyo devībhyo namaḥ

With these scented flowers oṃ I bow to All the Goddesses.

एते गन्धपुष्पे ॐ श्री गुरवे नमः

এতে গন্ধপুষ্পে ওঁ শ্রী গুরবে নমঃ

ete gandhapuṣpe oṃ śrī gurave namaḥ

With these scented flowers oṃ I bow to the Respected Guru.

दुर्गा पूजा   Durgā Pūjā

एते गन्धपुष्पे ॐ ब्राह्मणेभ्यो नमः

এতে গন্ধপুষ্পে ওঁ ব্রাহ্মণেভ্যো নমঃ

ete gandhapuṣpe oṃ brāhmaṇebhyo namaḥ
With these scented flowers oṃ I bow to All Knowers of Wisdom.

ācamana

Pour some water in right palm. Sip some water after each oṃ viṣṇu, then clean hands with remaining water and dry

ॐ विष्णु ॐ विष्णु ॐ विष्णु

ওঁ বিষ্ণু ওঁ বিষ্ণু ওঁ বিষ্ণু

oṃ viṣṇu oṃ viṣṇu oṃ viṣṇu
oṃ Consciousness, oṃ Consciousness, oṃ Consciousness

Draw the following yantra with some drops of water and/or sandal paste at the front of your seat. Place a flower on the bindu in the middle.

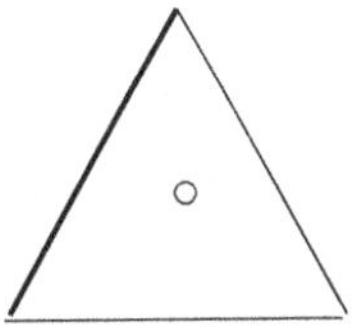

एते गन्धपुष्पे ॐ ह्रीं आधारशक्तये

कमलासनाय नमः ॥

এতে গন্ধপুষ্পে ওঁ হ্রীং আধারশক্তয়ে

কমলাসনায় নমঃ।।

ete gandhapuṣpe oṃ hrīṃ ādhāra śaktaye kamalāsanāya namaḥ
With these scented flowers oṃ hrīṃ I bow to the Primal Energy situated in this lotus seat.

Clap hands 3 times and snap fingers in the ten directions (N S E W NE SW NW SE UP DOWN) repeating **oṃ hrīṃ śrīṃ duṃ durgāyai namaḥ** *each time.*

ॐ ह्रीं श्रीं दुं दुर्गायै नमः

ওঁ হ্রীং শ্রীং দুং দুর্গায়ৈ নমঃ

दुर्गा पूजा Durgā Pūjā

oṃ hrīṃ śrīṃ duṃ durgāyai namaḥ

oṃ We bow to the Goddess, Durgā, the Grantor of Increase, who Removes all Difficulties.

Place a flower in left hand. Pour 3 drops of water on it after saying oṃ tat sat. *Place right hand over flower and finish reciting this verse with the appropriate names added (refer to a lunar calendar, if available), then offer the flower.*

विष्णुः ॐ तत् सत्। ॐ अद्य जम्बूद्वीपे ( ) देश ( ) प्रदेश ( ) नगरे ( ) मन्दिरे ( ) मासे ( ) पक्षे ( ) तिथौ ( ) गोत्र श्री ( ) कृतैतत् श्री दुर्गा कामः पूजा कर्माहं करिष्ये ॥

বিষ্ণুঃ ওঁ তৎ সৎ । ওঁ অদ্য জম্বূদ্বীপে ( ) দেশে ( ) প্রদেশে ( ) নগরে ( ) মন্দিরে ( ) মাসে ( ) পক্ষে ( ) তিথৌ ( ) গোত্র শ্রী ( ) কৃতৈতৎ শ্রী দূর্গা কামঃ পূজা কর্মাহং করিষ্যে ।।

viṣṇuḥ oṃ tat sat oṃ adya jambūdvīpe, (Country) deśe, (state) pradeśe, (City) nagare, (Divine Mother) mandire, (month) māse, (śukla or kriṣṇa) pakṣe, (name of day) tithau, name of (Satyānanda)} gotra, śrī (your name) kṛtaitat, śrī durgā kāmaḥ, pūjā karmāhaṃ kariṣye

The Consciousness Which Pervades All, oṃ That is Truth. Presently, on the Planet Earth, (America) Country, (Name) State, (Name) City, in (Devi Mandir) Temple, (Name of Month) Month, (Bright or Dark) fortnight, (Name of Day) Day, {Name of Sadhu Family (Satyānanda)}Gotra, Śrī (Your Name) is performing worship for the satisfaction of the Goddess, Durgā, the Grantor of Increase, who Removes all Difficulties.

दुर्गा पूजा Durgā Pūjā

Ring Bell

ॐ शान्ता द्यौ शान्ता पृथिवीं, शान्तमूर्ध्वमूर्वन्तरिक्षम् ।
शान्तमूध्वम्वतिरापः शान्तां नः शान्त्वोषधी ॥

ওঁ শান্তা দ্যৌ শান্তা পৃথিবীং, শান্তমূর্ধ্বমূর্বন্তরিক্ষম্ ।
শান্তমূর্ধ্বম্বতিরাপঃ শান্তাং নঃ শান্ত্বোষধী ।।

oṃ śāntā dyau śāntā pṛthivīṃ
śāntam ūrdhvam ūrvantarikṣam
śāntam ūrdhvam vatirāpaḥ śāntāṃ naḥ śāntvoṣadhī

oṃ Peace in the heavens, Peace on the earth, Peace upwards and permeating the atmosphere; Peace upwards, over, on all sides and further; Peace to us, Peace to all vegetation;

शान्ताणि पूर्वरूपाणि शान्तं नोऽस्तु कृताकृतम् ।
शान्तं भूतं च भव्यं च सर्वमेव समस्तु नः ॥

শান্তাণি পূর্বরূপাণি শান্তং নোহস্তু কৃতাকৃতম্ ।
শান্তং ভূতং চ ভব্যং চ সর্বমেব সমস্তু নঃ ।।

śāntāṇi pūrva rūpāṇi śāntaṃ no-stu kṛtā kṛtam
śāntaṃ bhūtaṃ ca bhavyaṃ ca sarvameva samastu naḥ

Peace to all that has form, Peace to all causes and effects; Peace to all existence, and to all intensities of reality including all and everything; Peace be to us.

पृथिवीं शान्तिरन्तरिक्षं शान्तिर्द्यौ । शान्तिरापः, शान्तिरोषधयः,
शान्तिः वनस्पतयः, शान्तिर्विश्वे मे देवाः, शान्तिः सर्व मे देवाः,
शान्तिर्ब्रह्म, शान्तिरापः, शान्ति सर्वम्, शान्तिरेधि, शान्तिः, शान्तिः,
सर्व शान्ति, सा मा शान्ति, शान्तिभिः ॥

পৃথিবীং শান্তিরন্তরিক্ষং শান্তির্দ্যৌ । শান্তিরাপঃ,
শান্তিরোষধয়ঃ, শান্তিঃ বনস্পতয়ঃ, শান্তির্বিশ্বে মে দেবাঃ,
শান্তিঃ সর্ব মে দেবাঃ, শান্তির্ব্রহ্ম, শান্তিরাপঃ, শান্তি সর্বম্,
শান্তিরেধি, শান্তিঃ, শান্তিঃ, সর্ব শান্তি, সা মা শান্তি,
শান্তিভিঃ ।।

pṛthivīṃ śāntir antarikṣaṃ śāntir dyau
śāntir āpaḥ, śāntir oṣadayaḥ, śāntiḥ vanaspatayaḥ, śāntir viśve me devāḥ, śāntiḥ sarva me devāḥ, śāntir brahma, śāntirāpaḥ, śānti sarvam, śāntiredhi, śāntiḥ, śāntiḥ, sarva śānti, sā mā śānti, śāntibhiḥ

Let the earth be at Peace, the atmosphere be at Peace, the heavens be filled with Peace. Even further may Peace extend, Peace to all vegetation, Peace to All Gods of the Universe, Peace to All Gods within me, Peace to Creative Consciousness, Peace be to Brilliant Light, Peace to All, Peace to Everything, Peace, Peace, altogether Peace, equally Peace, by means of Peace.

ॐ शान्तिः, शान्तिः, शान्तिः

ওঁ শান্তিঃ, শান্তিঃ, শান্তিঃ

oṃ śāntiḥ, śāntiḥ, śāntiḥ
oṃ Peace, Peace, Peace

Draw the following yantra on the plate or space for worship with sandal paste and/or water. Offer rice on the yantra for each of the next four mantras.

ॐ आधारशक्तये नमः

ওঁ আধারশক্তয়ে নমঃ

oṃ ādhāra śaktaye namaḥ
oṃ I bow to the Primal Energy

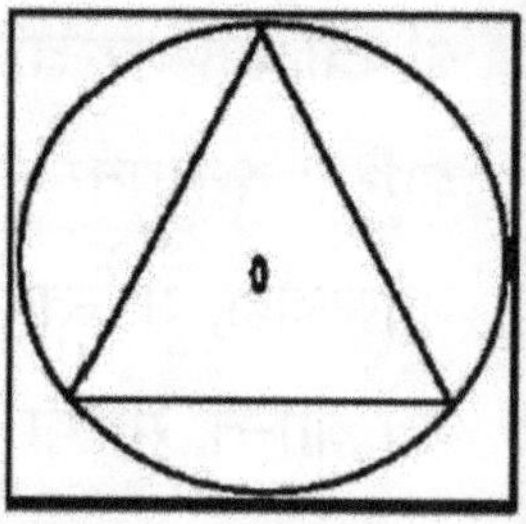

পৃথিবীং শান্তিরন্তরিক্ষং শান্তির্দ্যৌ । শান্তিরাপঃ,
শান্তিরোষধয়ঃ, শান্তিঃ বনস্পতয়ঃ, শান্তির্বিশ্বে মে দেবাঃ,
শান্তিঃ সর্ব মে দেবাঃ, শান্তির্ব্রহ্ম, শান্তিরাপঃ, শান্তি সর্বম্
শান্তিরেধি, শান্তিঃ, শান্তিঃ, সর্ব শান্তি, সা মা শান্তি,
শান্তিভিঃ ।।

pṛthivīṃ śāntir antarikṣaṃ śāntir dyau
śāntir āpaḥ, śāntir oṣadayaḥ, śāntiḥ vanaspatayaḥ, śāntir viśve me devāh, śāntiḥ sarva me devāḥ, śāntir brahma, śāntirāpaḥ, śānti sarvam, śāntiredhi, śāntiḥ, śāntiḥ, sarva śānti, sā mā śānti, śāntibhiḥ

Let the earth be at Peace, the atmosphere be at Peace, the heavens be filled with Peace. Even further may Peace extend, Peace to all vegetation, Peace to All Gods of the Universe, Peace to All Gods within me, Peace to Creative Consciousness, Peace be to Brilliant Light, Peace to All, Peace to Everything, Peace, Peace, altogether Peace, equally Peace, by means of Peace.

ॐ शान्तिः, शान्तिः, शान्तिः

ওঁ শান্তিঃ, শান্তিঃ, শান্তিঃ

oṃ śāntiḥ, śāntiḥ, śāntiḥ
oṃ Peace, Peace, Peace

Draw the following yantra on the plate or space for worship with sandal paste and/or water. Offer rice on the yantra for each of the next four mantras.

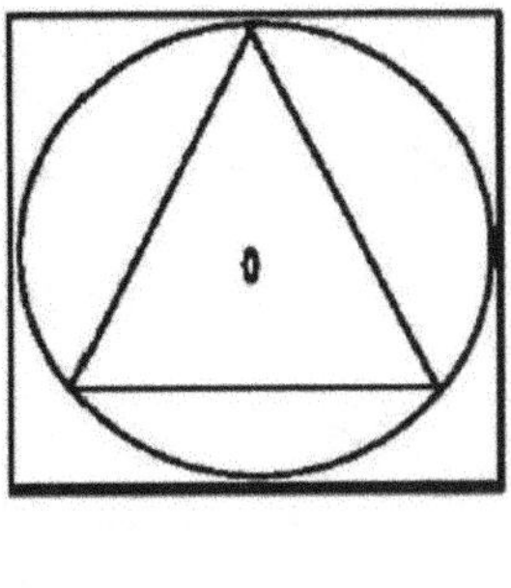

ॐ आधारशक्तये नमः

ওঁ আধারশক্তয়ে নমঃ

oṃ ādhāra śaktaye namaḥ
oṃ I bow to the Primal Energy

दुर्गा पूजा Durgā Pūjā

ॐ कुर्म्माय नमः

ওঁ কুর্ম্মায় নমঃ

oṃ kurmmāya namaḥ
oṃ I bow to the Support of the Earth

ॐ अनन्ताय नमः

ওঁ অনন্তায় নমঃ

oṃ anantāya namaḥ
oṃ I bow to Infinity

ॐ पृथिव्यै नमः

ওঁ পৃথিব্যৈ নমঃ

oṃ pṛthivyai namaḥ
oṃ I bow to the Earth

Place an empty water pot on the bindu in the center of the yantra when saying **phaṭ**

स्थां स्थीं स्थीरो भव फट्

স্থাং স্থীং স্থীরো ভব ফট্

sthāṃ sthīṃ sthīro bhava phaṭ
Be Still in the Gross Body! Be Still in the Subtle Body! Be Still in the Causal Body! PURIFY!

Fill pot with water while chanting mantra.

ॐ गङ्गे च यमुने चैव गोदावरि सरस्वति ।

नर्मदे सिन्धुकावेरि जलेऽस्मिन् सन्निधिं कुरु ॥

ওঁ গঙ্গে চ যমুনে চৈব গোদাবরি সরস্বতি ।

নর্মদে সিন্ধুকাবেরি জলেঽস্মিন্ সন্নিধিং কুরু ।।

दुर्गा पूजा   Durgā Pūjā

oṃ gaṅge ca yamune caiva godāvari sarasvati
narmade sindhu kāveri jale-asmin sannidhiṃ kuru
oṃ the Ganges, Yamuna, Godāvari, Saraswati, Narmada, Sindhu, Kāveri these waters are mingled together.

Note. The Ganges is the Iḍa, Yamuna is the Pingalā. The other five rivers are the five senses. The land of the seven rivers is within the body as well as outside.

Offer 3 flowers into the water pot with the mantra

एते गन्धपुष्पे ॐ ह्रीं श्रीं दुं दुर्गायै नमः

এতে গন্ধপুষ্পে ওঁ হ্রীং শ্রীং দুং দুর্গায়ৈ নমঃ

ete gandhapuṣpe oṃ hrīṃ śrīṃ duṃ durgāyai namaḥ
With these scented flowers oṃ We bow to the Goddess Durgā, the Grantor of Increase, who Removes all Difficulties.

Wave right hand in aṅkuṣa mudrā while chanting this mantra.

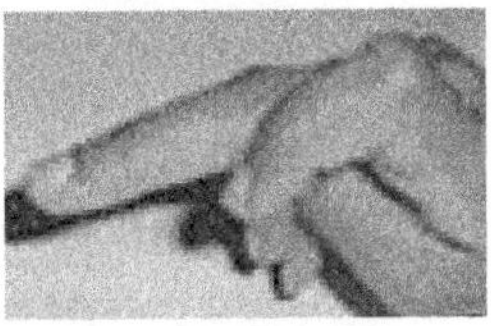

ॐ गङ्गे च यमुने चैव गोदावरि सरस्वति ।

नर्मदे सिन्धुकावेरि जलेऽस्मिन् सन्निधिं कुरु ॥

ওঁ গঙ্গে চ যমুনে চৈব গোদাবরি সরস্বতি ।

নর্মদে সিন্ধুকাবেরি জলেঽস্মিন্ সন্নিধিং কুরু ।।

oṃ gaṅge ca yamune caiva godāvari sarasvati
narmade sindhu kāveri jale-asmin sannidhiṃ kuru
oṃ the Ganges, Yamuna, Godāvari, Saraswati, Narmada, Sindhu, Kāveri these waters are mingled together.

ॐ ह्रीं श्रीं दुं दुर्गायै नमः   (Chant 10 times)

ওঁ হ্রীং শ্রীং দুং দুর্গায়ৈ নমঃ

oṃ hrīṃ śrīṃ duṃ durgāyai namaḥ
oṃ We bow to the Goddess Durgā, the Grantor of Increase, who Removes all Difficulties.

Sprinkle water over all articles to be offered, then throw some drops of water over your shoulders repeating the mantra:

अमृताम् कुरु स्वाहा

অমৃতাম্ কুরু স্বাহা

amritām kuru svāhā

Make this immortal nectar! I am One with God!

Puṣpa Śuddhi

Wave hands over flowers with prarthana mudrā while chanting first line and with dhenu mudrā while chanting second line of this mantra.

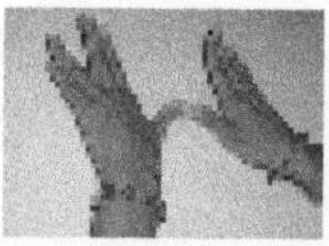

ॐ पुष्प पुष्प महापुष्प सुपुष्प पुष्पसम्भवे ।

पुष्प चयावकीर्णे च हूं फट् स्वाहा ॥

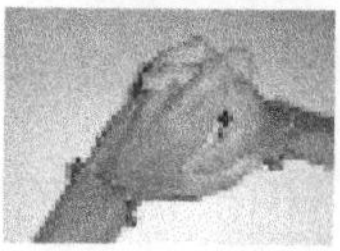

ওঁ পুষ্প পুষ্প মহাপুষ্প সুপুষ্প পুষ্পসম্ভবে ।

পুষ্প চয়াবকীর্ণে চ হুং ফট্ স্বাহা ।।

oṃ puṣpa puṣpa mahā puṣpa
supuṣpa puṣpasambhave
puṣpa cayāvakīrṇe ca hūṃ phaṭ svāhā

oṃ Flowers, flowers, Oh Great Flowers, excellent flowers; flowers in heaps and scattered about, cut the ego, purify, I am One with God!

Offer a flower while chanting each of the following mantras ete gandhapuṣpe

एते गन्धपुष्पे ॐ ह्रीं चण्डिकायै नमः

এতে গন্ধপুষ্পে ওঁ হ্রীং চণ্ডিকায়ৈ নমঃ

ete gandhapuṣpe oṃ hrīṃ caṇḍikāyai namaḥ

With these scented flowers oṃ I bow to She Who Tears Apart Thought

दुर्गा पूजा Durgā Pūjā

एते गन्धपुष्पे ॐ ह्रीं श्रीं दुं दुर्गायै नमः

এতে গন্ধপুষ্পে ওঁ হ্রীং শ্রীং দুং দুর্গায়ৈ নমঃ

ete gandhapuṣpe oṃ hrīṃ śrīṃ duṃ durgāyai namaḥ

With these scented flowers oṃ I bow to the Reliever of Difficulties

एते गन्धपुष्पे ॐ क्रीं काल्यै नमः

এতে গন্ধপুষ্পে ওঁ ক্রীং কাল্যৈ নমঃ

ete gandhapuṣpe oṃ krīṃ kālyai namaḥ

With these scented flowers oṃ I bow to the She Who Is Beyond Time (also the Goddess Who Takes Away Darkness)

एते गन्धपुष्पे ॐ श्रीं लक्ष्म्यै नमः

এতে গন্ধপুষ্পে ওঁ শ্রীং লক্ষ্ম্যৈ নমঃ

ete gandhapuṣpe oṃ śrīṃ lakṣmyai namaḥ

With these scented flowers oṃ I bow to the Goddess of True Wealth

एते गन्धपुष्पे ॐ सं सरस्वत्यै नमः

এতে গন্ধপুষ্পে ওঁ সং সরস্বত্যৈ নমঃ

ete gandhapuṣpe oṃ saṃ sarasvatyai namaḥ

With these scented flowers oṃ I bow to the Spirit of All-Pervading Knowledge

एते गन्धपुष्पे ॐ बौं ब्रह्मणे नमः

এতে গন্ধপুষ্পে ওঁ বৌং ব্রহ্মণে নমঃ

ete gandhapuṣpe oṃ bauṃ brahmaṇe namaḥ

With these scented flowers oṃ I bow to the Creative Consciousness

एते गन्धपुष्पे ॐ क्लीं विष्णवे नमः

এতে গন্ধপুষ্পে ওঁ ক্লীং বিষ্ণবে নমঃ

ete gandhapuṣpe oṃ klīṃ viṣṇave namaḥ

With these scented flowers oṃ I bow to the Consciousness Which Pervades All

एते गन्धपुष्पे ॐ नमः शिवाय

এতে গন্ধপুষ্পে ওঁ নমঃ শিবায়

ete gandhapuṣpe oṃ namaḥ śivāya

With these scented flowers oṃ I bow to the Consciousness of Infinite Goodness

dhyānam

meditation

ॐ जटाजूटसमायुक्तामर्द्धेन्दुकृतशेखराम् ।

लोचनत्रयसंयुक्तां पूर्णेन्दुसदृशाननाम् ॥

ওঁ জটাজূটসমায়ুক্তামর্দ্ধেন্দুকৃতশেখরাম্ ।

লোচনত্রয়সংযুক্তাং পূর্ণেন্দুসদৃশাননাম্ ।।

oṃ jaṭājūṭasamāyuktāmarddhendukṛtaśekharām
locanatrayasaṃyuktāṃ pūrṇendusadṛśānanām

Oṃ With loose flowing tresses, poised with equanimity with the radiant half moon upon her head, her three eyes are shining like the full moon.

तप्तकाञ्चनवर्णाभां सुप्रतिष्ठां सुलोचनाम् ।

नवयौवनसम्पन्नां सर्वाभरणभूषिताम् ॥

তপ্তকাঞ্চনবর্ণাভাং সুপ্রতিষ্ঠাং সুলোচনাম্ ।

নবয়ৌবনসম্পন্নাং সর্বাভরণভূষিতাম্ ।।

taptakāñcanavarṇābhāṃ supratiṣṭāṃ sulocanām
navayauvanasampannāṃ sarvābharaṇabhūṣitām

She has the color of melted gold, of excellent birth and beautiful eyes. She has nine manifestations all resplendantly shining with their ornaments.

सुचारुदशनां तद्वत् पीनोन्नतपयोधराम् ।
त्रिभङ्गस्थानसंस्थानां महिषासुरमर्दिनीम् ॥

সুচারুদশনাং তদ্বৎ পীনোন্নতপয়োধরাম্ ।
ত্রিভঙ্গস্থানসংস্থানাং মহিষাসুরমর্দিনীম্ ।।

sucārudaśanāṃ tadvat pīnonnatapayodharām
tribhaṅgasthānasaṃsthānāṃ mahiṣāsuramardinīm

She holds aloft ten excellent weapons in her hands, and has three beautiful folds under her breasts - the Slayer of the Great Ego.

मृणालायतसंस्पर्श दशबाहु समन्विताम् ।
त्रिशूलं दक्षिणे ध्येयं खड्गं चक्रं क्रमादधः ॥

মৃণালায়তসংস্পর্শ দশবাহু সমন্বিতাম্ ।
ত্রিশূলং দক্ষিণে ধ্যেয়ং খড়্গং চক্রং ক্রমাদধঃ ।।

mṛṇālāyatasaṃsparśa daśabāhu samanvitām
triśūlaṃ dakṣiṇe dhyeyaṃ khaḍgaṃ cakraṃ kramādadhaḥ

She bears the touch of death to the Ego in each of her ten arms. We meditate on the order of weapons beginning at the upper right: trident, sword, discus,

तीक्ष्नबाणं तथा शक्तिं दक्षिणेषु विचिन्तयेत् ।
खेटकं पूर्णचापञ्च पाशमङ्कुशमेव च ॥

তীক্ষ্নবাণং তথা শক্তিং দক্ষিণেষু বিচিন্তয়েৎ ।
খেটকং পূর্ণচাপঞ্চ পাশমঙ্কুশমেব চ ।।

tīkṣṇabāṇaṃ tathā śaktiṃ dakṣiṇeṣu vicintayet
kheṭakaṃ pūrṇacāpañca pāśamaṅkuśameva ca
bow and arrow, and then energy we contemplate on her right side. Shield, club, noose, and curved sword,

घण्टां वा परशु वापि वामतः सन्निवेशयेत् ।
अधस्तान्महिषं तद्वद्विशिरस्कं प्रदर्शयेत् ॥

ঘণ্টাং বা পরশু বাপি বামতঃ সন্নিবেশয়েৎ ।
অধস্তান্মহিষং তদ্বদ্বিশিরস্কং প্রদর্শয়েৎ ।।

ghaṇṭāṃ vā paraśu vāpi vāmataḥ sanniveśayet
adhastānmahiṣaṃ tadvadviśiraskaṃ pradarśayet
the bell or the battle-axe, we contemplate on her left side. Below lies the severed head of the Great Ego in the form of a buffalo.

शिरश्छेदोद्भवं तद्वद्दानवं खड्गपाणिनम् ।
हृदि शूलेन निर्भिन्नं निर्जदन्त्रविभूषितम् ॥

শিরশ্ছেদোদ্ভবং তদ্বদ্দানবং খড়্গাপাণিনম্ ।
হৃদি শূলেন নির্ভিন্নং নির্যদন্ত্রবিভূষিতম্ ।।

śiraśchedodbhavaṃ tadvaddānavaṃ khaḍgāpāṇinam
hṛdi śūlena nirbhinnaṃ nirjadantravibhūṣitam
In place of the severed head on his neck is the demonic image of the Great Ego with a sword in his hand. He is shown gritting his teeth from the spear which has pierced his heart.

रक्तारक्तीकृताङ्गञ्च रक्तविस्फूरितेक्षणम् ।
वेष्ठितं नागपाशेन भ्रूकुटीभीषणाननम् ॥

রক্তারক্তীকৃতাঙ্গঞ্চ রক্তবিস্ফূরিতেক্ষণম্ ।
বেষ্ঠিতং নাগপাশেন ভ্রূকুটীভীষণাননম্ ।।

raktāraktīkṛtāṅgañca raktavisphūritekṣaṇam
veṣṭhitaṃ nāgapāśena bhrūkuṭībhīṣaṇānanam

Blood is flowing over his body and red is seen on all his limbs. The cobra snake in the form of a noose has wrapped itself around his brow and upper left arm.

सपाशवामहस्तेन धृतकेशन्तु दुर्गया ।

वमद्रुधिरवक्त्रञ्च देव्याः सिंहं प्रदर्शयेत् ॥

সপাশবামহস্তেন ধৃতকেশন্তু দুর্গয়া ।

বমদ্রুধিরবক্ত্রঞ্চ দেব্যাঃ সিংহং প্রদর্শয়েৎ ।।

sapāśavāmahastena dhṛtakeśantu durgayā
vamadrudhiravaktrañca devyāḥ siṃhaṃ pradarśayet

On the side of the Goddess is shown the lion, Dharma, who is her conveyance, and is facing the left.

देव्यास्तु दक्षिणं पादं समं सिंहोपरि स्थितम् ।

किञ्चिदूर्द्धं तथा वाममङ्गुष्ठं महिषोपरि ॥

দেব্যাস্তু দক্ষিণং পাদং সমং সিংহোপরি স্থিতম্ ।

কিঞ্চিদূর্দ্ধং তথা বামমঙ্গুষ্ঠং মহিষোপরি ।।

devyāstu dakṣiṇaṃ pādaṃ samaṃ siṃhopari sthitam
kiñcidūrddhaṃ tathā vāmamaṅguṣṭhaṃ mahiṣopari

The Goddess's right foot is flatly positioned on top of the lion. A little elevated only her left toe is on top of the Great Ego.

प्रसन्नवदनां देवीं सर्वकामफलप्रदां ।

स्तुयमानञ्च तद्रूपममरैः सन्निवेशयेत् ॥

প্রসন্নবদনাং দেবীং সর্বকামফলপ্রদাং ।

স্তুয়মানঞ্চ তদ্রূপমমরৈঃ সন্নিবেশয়েৎ ।।

prasannavadanāṃ devīṃ sarvakāmaphalapradāṃ
stuyamānañca tadrūpamamaraiḥ sanniveśayet

The Goddess is extremely pleased and grants the fruits of all desires to those who contemplate her excellent form and with one mind sing her praises:

ऊग्रचण्डा प्रचण्डा च चण्डोग्रा चण्डनायिका ।
चण्डा चण्डवती चैव चण्डरूपातिचण्डिका ॥

উগ্রচণ্ডা প্রচণ্ডা চ চণ্ডোগ্রা চণ্ডনায়িকা ।
চণ্ডা চণ্ডবতী চৈব চণ্ডরূপাতিচণ্ডিকা ।।

ūgracaṇḍā pracaṇḍā ca caṇḍogrā caṇḍanāyikā
caṇḍā caṇḍavatī caiva caṇḍarūpāticaṇḍikā

The Terrible Slayer of Passion, Whose Nature Removes Fear, She Who Slays Fear, She Who Sees Everywhere Freedom from Fear, She Who Tears Apart Fear, She Who Contains Fearlessness, The Form of the Erradicator of Fear, and the Primary She Who Tears Apart All Thoughts.

अष्टाभिः शक्तिभिस्ताभिः सततं परिवेष्ठिताम् ।
चिन्तयेज्ज्गतां धात्रीं धर्म्मकामार्थमोक्षदाम् ॥

অষ্টাভিঃ শক্তিভিস্তাভিঃ সততং পরিবেষ্ঠিতাম্ ।
চিন্তয়েজ্জগতাং ধাত্রীং ধর্ম্মকামার্থমোক্ষদাম্ ।।

aṣṭābhiḥ śaktibhistābhiḥ satataṃ pariveṣṭhitām
cintayejjagatāṃ dhātrīṃ dharmmakāmārthamokṣadām

With these eight energies always surrounding her, we think of the Creator of the Perceivable Universe, who bestows the Way of Truth and Harmony, Satiation of Desires, Material Sustenance, and Liberation otherwise known as Self-Realization.

kara nyāsa

establishment in the hands

ॐ ह्रां अंगुष्ठाभ्यां नमः

ওঁ হ্রাং অঙ্গুষ্ঠাভ্যাং নমঃ

oṃ hrāṃ aṅguṣṭhābhyāṃ namaḥ *thumb/forefinger*

oṃ hrāṃ in the thumb I bow.

ॐ ह्रीं तर्जनीभ्यां स्वाहा

ওঁ হ্রীং তর্জনীভ্যাং স্বাহা

oṃ hrīṃ tarjanībhyāṃ svāhā *thumb/forefinger*

oṃ **hrīṃ** in the forefinger, I am One with God!

ॐ ह्रूं मध्यमाभ्यां वषट्

ওঁ হ্রূং মধ্যমাভ্যাং বষট্

oṃ hrūṃ madhyamābhyāṃ vaṣaṭ *thumb/middle finger*

oṃ hrūṃ in the middle finger, Purify!

ॐ ह्रैं अनामिकाभ्यां हुं

ওঁ হ্রৈং অনামিকাভ্যাং হুং

oṃ hraiṃ anāmikābhyāṃ huṃ *thumb/ring finger*

oṃ hraiṃ in the ring finger, Cut the Ego!

ॐ ह्रौं कनिष्ठिकाभ्यां वौषट्

ওঁ হ্রৌং কনিষ্ঠিকাভ্যাং বৌষট্

oṃ hrauṃ kaniṣṭhikābhyāṃ vauṣaṭ *thumb/little finger*

oṃ hrauṃ in the little finger, Ultimate Purity!

Roll hand over hand forwards while reciting karatala kara, and backwards while chanting pṛṣṭhābhyāṃ, then clap hands when chanting astrāya phaṭ.

ॐ ह्रः करतल कर पृष्ठाभ्यां अस्त्राय फट् ॥

ওঁ হ্রঃ করতল কর পৃষ্ঠাভ্যাং অস্ত্রায় ফট্ ।।

oṃ hraḥ karatala kara pṛṣṭhābhyāṃ astrāya phaṭ

Oṃ hraḥ I bow to the Goddess Durgā, with the weapon of Virtue.

ॐ ह्रीं श्रीं दुं दुर्गायै नमः

ওঁ হ্রীং শ্রীং দুং দুর্গায়ৈ নমঃ

oṃ hrīṃ śrīṃ duṃ durgāyai namaḥ

Oṃ I bow to the Goddess, Durgā, the Grantor of Increase, who Removes all Difficulties

aṅga nyāsa
establishment in the body

Holding tattva mudrā, touch heart.

ॐ ह्रां हृदयाय नमः

ওঁ হ্রাং হৃদয়ায় নমঃ

oṃ hrāṃ hṛdayāya namaḥ *touch heart*

Oṃ hrāṃ in the heart, I bow.

Holding tattva mudrā, touch top of head.

ॐ ह्रीं शिरसे स्वाहा

ওঁ হ্রীং শিরসে স্বাহা

oṃ hrīṃ śirase svāhā *top of head*

Oṃ hrīṃ on the top of the head, I am One with God!

With thumb extended, touch back of head.

ॐ ह्रूं शिखायै वषट्

ওঁ হ্রূং শিখায়ৈ বষট্

oṃ hrūṃ śikhāyai vaṣaṭ *back of head*

Oṃ hrūṃ on the back of the head, Purify!

दुर्गा पूजा Durgā Pūjā

Holding tattva mudrā, cross both arms.

ॐ हैं कवचाय हुं

ওঁ হৈং কবচায় হুং

oṃ hraiṃ kavacāya huṃ *cross both arms*

Oṃ hraiṃ crossing both arms, Cut the Ego!

Holding tattva mudrā, touch three eyes at once with three middle fingers.

ॐ ह्रौं नेत्रत्रयाय वौषट्

ওঁ হ্রৌং নেত্রত্রয়ায় বৌষট্

oṃ hrauṃ netratrayāya vauṣaṭ *touch three eyes*

Oṃ hrauṃ in the three eyes, Ultimate Purity!

Roll hand over hand forwards while reciting karatala kara, and backwards while chanting pṛṣṭhābhyāṃ, then clap hands when chanting astrāya phaṭ.

ॐ ह्रः करतल कर पृष्ठाभ्यां अस्त्राय फट् ॥

ওঁ হ্রঃ করতল কর পৃষ্ঠাভ্যাং অস্ত্রায় ফট্ ।।

oṃ hraḥ karatala kara pṛṣṭhābhyāṃ astrāya phaṭ

Oṃ hraḥ I bow to the Goddess Durgā, with the weapon of Virtue.

ॐ ह्रीं श्रीं दुं दुर्गायै नमः

ওঁ হ্রীং শ্রীং দুং দুর্গায়ৈ নমঃ

oṃ hrīṃ śrīṃ duṃ durgāyai namaḥ

Oṃ I bow to the Goddess Durgā, the Grantor of Increase, who Removes all Difficulties

अथ दुर्गाद्वात्रिंशन्नाममाला

অথ দুর্গাদ্বাত্রিংশন্নামমালা

atha durgā dvātriṃśannāma mālā
The Rosary of Thirty-two Names of Durgā

दुर्गा दुर्गार्तिशमनी दुर्गापद्विनिवारिणी ।
दुर्गमच्छेदिनी दुर्गसाधिनी दुर्गनाशिनी ॥

দুর্গা দুর্গার্তিশমনী দুর্গাপদ্বিনিবারিণী ।
দুর্গমচ্ছেদিনী দুর্গসাধিনী দুর্গনাশিনী ।।

durgā durgārti śamanī durgā padvinivāriṇī
durgamacchedinī durga sādhinī durga nāśinī

1. The Reliever of Difficulties
2. Who Puts Difficulties at Peace
3. Dispeller of Difficult Adversities
4. Who Cuts Down Difficulties
5. The Performer of Discipline to Expel Difficulties
6. The Destroyer of Difficulties

दुर्गतोद्धारिणी दुर्गनिहन्त्री दुर्गमापहा ।
दुर्गमज्ञानदा दुर्गदैत्यलोकदवानला ॥

দুর্গতোদ্ধারিণী দুর্গনিহন্ত্রী দুর্গমাপহা ।
দুর্গমজ্ঞানদা দুর্গদৈত্যলোকদবানলা ।।

durgatod dhāriṇī durga nihantrī durga māpahā
durgamajñānadā durga daityaloka davānalā

7. Who Holds the Whip to Difficulties
8. Who Sends Difficulties to Ruin
9. Who Measures Difficulties
10. Who Makes Difficulties Unconscious
11. Who Destroys the World of Difficult Thoughts

दुर्गमा दुर्गमालोका दुर्गमात्मस्वरूपिणी ।

दुर्गमार्गप्रदा दुर्गमविद्या दुर्गमाश्रिता ॥

দুর্গমা দুর্গমালোকা দুর্গমাত্মস্বরূপিণী ।

দুর্গমার্গপ্রদা দুর্গমবিদ্যা দুর্গমাশ্রিতা ।।

durgamā durgamālokā durgamātmasvarūpiṇī
durgamārgapradā durgam avidyā durgamāśritā

12. The Mother of Difficulties
13. The Perception of Difficulties
14. The Intrinsic Nature of the Soul of Difficulties
15. Who Searches Through Difficulties
16. The Knowledge of Difficulties
17. The Extrication From Difficulties

दुर्गमज्ञानसंस्थाना दुर्गमध्यानभासिनी ।

दुर्गमोहा दुर्गमगा दुर्गमार्थस्वरूपिणी ॥

দুর্গমজ্ঞানসংস্থানা দুর্গমধ্যানভাসিনী ।

দুর্গমোহা দুর্গমগা দুর্গমার্থস্বরূপিণী ।।

durgam ajñāna saṃsthānā durgam adhyāna bhāsinī
durga mohā durgamagā durgamārtha svarūpiṇī

18. The Continued Existence of Difficulties
19. Whose Meditation Remains Brilliant When in Difficulties
20. Who Deludes Difficulties
21. Who Resolves Difficulties
22. Who is the Intrinsic Nature of the Object of Difficulties

दुर्गमासुरसंहन्त्री दुर्गमायुधधारिणी ।

दुर्गमाङ्गी दुर्गमता दुर्गम्या दुर्गमेश्वरी ॥

দুর্গমাসুরসংহন্ত্রী দুর্গমায়ুধধারিণী ।

দুর্গমাঙ্গী দুর্গমতা দুর্গম্যা দুর্গমেশ্বরী ।।

durgam āsura saṃhantrī durgam āyudha dhāriṇī
durgamāṅgī durgamatā durgamyā durgameśvarī

23. The Annihilator of the Egotism of Difficulties
24. Bearer of the Weapon Against Difficulties
25. The Refinery of Difficulties
26. Who is Beyond Difficulties
27. This Present Difficulty
28. The Empress of Difficulties

दुर्गभीमा दुर्गभामा दुर्गभा दुर्गदारिणी ।
नामावलिमिमां यस्तु दुर्गाया मम मानवः ।

দুর্গভীমা দুর্গভামা দুর্গভা দুর্গদারিণী ।
নামাবলিমিমাং য়স্তু দুর্গায়া মম মানবঃ ।

durgabhīmā durgabhāmā durgabhā durgadāriṇī
nāmāvalimimāṃ yastu durgāyā mama mānavaḥ

29. Who is Terrible to Difficulties
30. The Lady of Difficulties
31. The Illuminator of Difficulties
32. Who Cuts Off Difficulties

Whoever will recite this garland of the names of Durgā,

पठेत् सर्वभयान्मुक्तो भविष्यति न संशयः ॥

পঠেৎ সর্বভয়ান্মুক্তো ভবিষ্যতি ন সংশয়ঃ ।।

paṭhet sarva bhayānmukto bhaviṣyati na saṃśayaḥ

the Reliever of Difficulties, for me, will be freed from every type of fear without a doubt.

ॐ ह्रीं श्रीं दुं दुर्गायै नमः

ওঁ হ্রীং শ্রীং দুং দুর্গায়ৈ নমঃ

oṃ hrīṃ śrīṃ duṃ durgāyai namaḥ (108 times)

We bow to the Goddess, Durgā, the Grantor of Increase, who Removes all Difficulties

दुर्गा पूजा Durgā Pūjā

If desired, collect the next eight liquid offerings in a bowl.

foot bath

ॐ ह्रीं श्रीं दुं दुर्गायै नमः पाद्यं समर्पयामि ॥

ওঁ হ্রীং শ্রীং দুং দুর্গায়ৈ নমঃ পাদ্যং সমর্পয়ামি ।।

oṃ hrīṃ śrīṃ duṃ durgāyai namaḥ pādyaṃ samarpayāmi

oṃ We bow to the Goddess, Durgā, the Grantor of Increase, who Removes all Difficulties, and offer these foot bath waters.

milk bath

ॐ ह्रीं श्रीं दुं दुर्गायै नमः पयः स्नानं समर्पयामि ॥

ওঁ হ্রীং শ্রীং দুং দুর্গায়ৈ নমঃ পয়ঃ স্নানং সমর্পয়ামি ।।

oṃ hrīṃ śrīṃ duṃ durgāyai namaḥ payaḥ snānaṃ samarpayāmi

oṃ We bow to the Goddess, Durgā, the Grantor of Increase, who Removes all Difficulties, and offer this milk for your bath.

yogurt bath

ॐ ह्रीं श्रीं दुं दुर्गायै नमः दधि स्नानं समर्पयामि ॥

ওঁ হ্রীং শ্রীং দুং দুর্গায়ৈ নমঃ দধি স্নানং সমর্পয়ামি ।।

oṃ hrīṃ śrīṃ duṃ durgāyai namaḥ dadhi snānaṃ samarpayāmi

oṃ We bow to the Goddess, Durgā, the Grantor of Increase, who Removes all Difficulties, and offer this curd for your bath.

ghee bath

ॐ ह्रीं श्रीं दुं दुर्गायै नमः घृत स्नानं समर्पयामि ॥

ওঁ হ্রীং শ্রীং দুং দুর্গায়ৈ নমঃ ঘৃত স্নানং সমর্পয়ামি ।।

oṃ hrīṃ śrīṃ duṃ durgāyai namaḥ ghṛta snānaṃ samarpayāmi

oṃ We bow to the Goddess, Durgā, the Grantor of Increase, who Removes all Difficulties, and offer this ghee for your bath.

honey bath

ॐ ह्रीं श्रीं दुं दुर्गायै नमः मधु स्नानं समर्पयामि ॥

ওঁ হ্রীং শ্রীং দুং দুর্গায়ৈ নমঃ মধু স্নানং সমর্পয়ামি ।।

oṃ hrīṃ śrīṃ duṃ durgāyai namaḥ madhu snānaṃ samarpayāmi

oṃ We bow to the Goddess, Durgā, the Grantor of Increase, who Removes all Difficulties, and offer this honey for your bath.

sugar bath

ॐ ह्रीं श्रीं दुं दुर्गायै नमः शर्करा स्नानं समर्पयामि ॥

ওঁ হ্রীং শ্রীং দুং দুর্গায়ৈ নমঃ শর্করা স্নানং সমর্পয়ামি ।।

oṃ hrīṃ śrīṃ duṃ durgāyai namaḥ śarkarā snānaṃ samarpayāmi

oṃ We bow to the Goddess, Durgā, the Grantor of Increase, who Removes all Difficulties, and offer this sugar for your bath.

five nectars bath

ॐ ह्रीं श्रीं दुं दुर्गायै नमः पञ्चामृतं स्नानं समर्पयामि ॥

ওঁ হ্রীং শ্রীং দুং দুর্গায়ৈ নমঃ পঞ্চামৃতং স্নানং সমর্পয়ামি ।।

oṃ hrīṃ śrīṃ duṃ durgāyai namaḥ pañcāmṛtaṃ snānaṃ samarpayāmi

oṃ We bow to the Goddess, Durgā, the Grantor of Increase, who Removes all Difficulties, and offer these five nectars for your bath.

water bath

ॐ ह्रीं श्रीं दुं दुर्गायै नमः गङ्गा स्नानं समर्पयामि ॥

ওঁ হ্রীং শ্রীং দুং দুর্গায়ৈ নমঃ গঙ্গা স্নানং সমর্পয়ামি ।।

oṃ hrīṃ śrīṃ duṃ durgāyai namaḥ gaṅgā snānaṃ samarpayāmi

oṃ We bow to the Goddess, Durgā, the Grantor of Increase, who Removes all Difficulties, and offer these bath waters.

cloth

ॐ ह्रीं श्रीं दुं दुर्गायै नमः वस्त्रां समर्पयामि ॥

ওঁ হ্রীং শ্রীং দুং দুর্গায়ৈ নমঃ বস্ত্রাং সমর্পয়ামি ।।

oṃ hrīṃ śrīṃ duṃ durgāyai namaḥ vastrāṃ samarpayāmi

oṃ We bow to the Goddess, Durgā, the Grantor of Increase, who Removes all Difficulties, and offer this wearing apparel.

rudrākṣa

ॐ ह्रीं श्रीं दुं दुर्गायै नमः रुद्राक्षं समर्पयामि ॥

ওঁ হ্রীং শ্রীং দুং দুর্গায়ৈ নমঃ রুদ্রাক্ষং সমর্পয়ামি ।।

oṃ hrīṃ śrīṃ duṃ durgāyai namaḥ rudrākṣaṃ samarpayāmi

oṃ We bow to the Goddess, Durgā, the Grantor of Increase, who Removes all Difficulties, and offer this rudrākṣa.

red powder

ॐ ह्रीं श्रीं दुं दुर्गायै नमः सिन्दूरं समर्पयामि ॥

ওঁ হ্রীং শ্রীং দুং দুর্গায়ৈ নমঃ সিন্দূরং সমর্পয়ামি ।।

oṃ hrīṃ śrīṃ duṃ durgāyai namaḥ sindūraṃ samarpayāmi

oṃ We bow to the Goddess, Durgā, the Grantor of Increase, who Removes all Difficulties, and offer this red colored powder.

sandal paste

ॐ ह्रीं श्रीं दुं दुर्गायै नमः चन्दनं समर्पयामि ॥

ওঁ হ্রীং শ্রীং দুং দুর্গায়ৈ নমঃ চন্দনং সমর্পয়ামি ।।

oṃ hrīṃ śrīṃ duṃ durgāyai namaḥ candanaṃ samarpayāmi

oṃ We bow to the Goddess, Durgā, the Grantor of Increase, who Removes all Difficulties, and offer this sandal paste.

rice

ॐ ह्रीं श्रीं दुं दुर्गायै नमः अक्षतं समर्पयामि ॥

ওঁ হ্রীং শ্রীং দুং দুর্গায়ৈ নমঃ অক্ষতং সমর্পয়ামি ।।

oṃ hrīṃ śrīṃ duṃ durgāyai namaḥ akṣataṃ samarpayāmi

oṃ We bow to the Goddess, Durgā, the Grantor of Increase, who Removes all Difficulties, and offer these grains of rice.

flower garland

ॐ ह्रीं श्रीं दुं दुर्गायै नमः पुष्पमालां समर्पयामि ॥

ওঁ হ্রীং শ্রীং দুং দুর্গায়ৈ নমঃ পুষ্পমালাং সমর্পয়ামি ।।

oṃ hrīṃ śrīṃ duṃ durgāyai namaḥ puṣpamālāṃ samārpāyāmi

oṃ We bow to the Goddess, Durgā, the Grantor of Increase, who Removes all Difficulties, and offer this garland of flowers.

food offering

ॐ ह्रीं श्रीं दुं दुर्गायै नमः भोग नैवेद्यम् समर्पयामि ॥

ওঁ হ্রীং শ্রীং দুং দুর্গায়ৈ নমঃ ভোগ নৈবেদ্যম্ সমর্পয়ামি ।।

oṃ hrīṃ śrīṃ duṃ durgāyai namaḥ bhog naivedyam samarpayāmi

oṃ We bow to the Goddess, Durgā, the Grantor of Increase, who Removes all Difficulties, and offer this presentation of food.

drinking water

ॐ ह्रीं श्रीं दुं दुर्गायै नमः पानार्थ जलम् समर्पयामि ॥

ওঁ হ্রীং শ্রীং দুং দুর্গায়ৈ নমঃ পানার্থ জলম্ সমর্পয়ামি ।।

oṃ hrīṃ śrīṃ duṃ durgāyai namaḥ pānārtha jalam samarpayāmi

oṃ We bow to the Goddess, Durgā, the Grantor of Increase, who Removes all Difficulties, and offer this drinking water.

एते गन्धपुष्पे ॐ ह्रीं श्रीं दुं दुर्गायै नमः

এতে গন্ধপুষ্পে ওঁ হ্রীং শ্রীং দুং দুর্গায়ৈ নমঃ

ete gandha puṣpe oṃ hrīṃ śrīṃ duṃ durgāyai namaḥ
With these scented flowers oṃ We bow to the Goddess, Durgā, the Grantor of Increase, who Removes all Difficulties.

ॐ ह्रीं श्रीं दुं दुर्गायै नमः

ওঁ হ্রীং শ্রীং দুং দুর্গায়ৈ নমঃ

oṃ hrīṃ śrīṃ duṃ durgāyai namaḥ (108 times)
We bow to the Goddess, Durgā, the Grantor of Increase, who Removes all Difficulties.

ॐ प्रथमं शैलपुत्री च द्वितीयं ब्रह्मचारिणी ।

तृतीयं चन्द्रघण्टेति कूष्माण्डेति चतुर्थकम् ॥

ওঁ প্রথমং শৈলপুত্রী চ দ্বিতীয়ং ব্রহ্মচারিণী ।

তৃতীয়ং চন্দ্রঘণ্টেতি কূষ্মাণ্ডেতি চতুর্থকম্ ।।

oṃ prathamaṃ śailaputrī ca dvitīyaṃ brahmacāriṇī
tṛtīyaṃ candraghaṇṭeti kūṣmāṇḍeti caturthakam
oṃ First is the Goddess of Inspiration, and second the Goddess of Sacred Study; third is the Goddess of the Delight of Practice, the Goddess of Purifying Austerity is fourth.

पञ्चमं स्कन्दमातेति षष्ठं कात्यायनीति च ।

सप्तमं कालरात्रीति महागौरीति चाष्टमम् ॥

পঞ্চমং স্কন্দমাতেতি ষষ্ঠং কাত্যায়নীতি চ ।

সপ্তমং কালরাত্রীতি মহাগৌরীতি চাষ্টমম্ ।।

pañcamaṃ skandamāteti ṣaṣṭhaṃ kātyāyanīti ca
saptamaṃ kālarātrīti mahāgaurīti cāṣṭamam
Fifth is the Goddess who Nurtures Divinity, sixth is the One Who is Ever-Pure and Free from Error; seventh is the Goddess of the Dark Night of Overcoming Egotism, the Goddess of the Great Radiant Light is eighth.

नवमं सिद्धिदात्री च नवदुर्गाः प्रकीर्तिताः ।
उक्तान्येतानि नामानि ब्रह्मणैव महात्मना ॥

নবমং সিদ্ধিদাত্রী চ নবদুর্গাঃ প্রকীর্তিতাঃ ।
উক্তান্যেতানি নামানি ব্রহ্মণৈব মহাত্মনা ।।

navamaṃ siddhidātrī ca navadurgāḥ prakīrtitāḥ
uktānyetāni nāmāni brahmaṇaiva mahātmanā

Ninth is the Goddess who Grants Perfection, the nine Durgās, Relievers of Difficulties, have been enumerated, and these names have been revealed by the great soul of the Supreme himself.

Śrī Durgā Cālīsā

The Adventures of Durgā

दोहा

দোহা

dohā

जय श्री दुर्गा अम्बिका, जगत्पालिनी माता ।
तुम्हरो चालीसा रचहुँ, कीजै मोहि सनाथ ॥

জয় শ্রী দুর্গা অম্বিকা, জগৎপালিনী মাতা ।
তুম্হরো চালীসা রচহুঁ, কীজৈ মোহি সনাথ ।।

jaya śrī durgā ambikā, jagatpālinī mātā
tumharo cālīsā racahuṁ, kījai mohi sanātha

Victory to the Respected Reliever of Difficulties, Mother of the Universe, the Mother who protects the world. I elucidate your song of praise. Please eradicate all ignorance.

श्री दुर्गा माता कि जय

শ্রী দুর্গা মাতা কি জয়

śrī durgā mātā ki jaya

Victory to the respected Durgā Mā

दुर्गा पूजा Durgā Pūjā

नमो नमो दुर्गे सुख करनी ।

नमो नमो अम्बे दुख हरनी ॥

নমো নমো দুর্গে সুখ করনী ।

নমো নমো অম্বে দুখ হরনী ।।

namo namo durge sukha karanī
namo namo ambe dukha haranī

I bow, I bow, to the Reliever of Difficulties, Cause of Happiness.
I bow, I bow, to the Mother who takes away all pain.

निरंकार है ज्योति तुम्हारी ।

तिहूँ लोक फैली उजियारी ॥

নিরংকার হৈ জ্যোতি তুম্হারী ।

তিহূঁ লোক ফৈলী উজিয়ারী ।।

niraṃkāra hai jyoti tumhārī
tihūṁ loka phailī ujiyārī

Your light illuminates all darkness, your brightness extends over the three worlds.

शशि ललाट मुख विशाला ।

नेत्र लाल भृकुटी विकराला ॥

শশি ললাট মুখ বিশালা ।

নেত্র লাল ভৃকুটী বিকরালা ।।

śaśi lalāṭa mukha viśālā
netra lāla bhṛkuṭī vikarālā

With the moon on your forehead your face is tremendous. When you frown with red eyes it is terribly frightening.

रूप मातु को अति सुहवै ।

दरश करत जन अति सुख पावै ॥

রূপ মাতু কো অতি সুহবৈ ।

দরশ করত জন অতি সুখ পাবৈ ।।

rūpa mātu ko ati suhavai
daraśa karata jana ati sukha pāvai

In the form of Mother it is extremely pleasing, and those who see you in this way receive the greatest pleasure.

तुम संसार शक्ति लै कीन्हा ।

पालन हेतु अन्नधन दीन्हा ॥

তুম সংসার শক্তি লৈ কীন্হা ।

পালন হেতু অন্নধন দীন্হা ।।

tuma saṃsāra śakti lai kīnhā
pālana hetu annadhana dīnhā

You move all the energy amongst all objects and relationships. You protect all, and are the Giver of grains and wealth.

अन्नपूर्णा तुम जग पाला ।

तुमहीं आदि सुन्दरी बाला ॥

অন্নপূর্ণা তুম জগ পালা ।

তুমহীং আদি সুন্দরী বালা ।।

annapūrṇā tuma jaga pālā
tumahīṃ ādi sundarī bālā

As the Goddess who is full of grains and food you protect the world. You are the foremost and most beautiful being.

प्रलयकाल सब नाशन हारी ।

तुम गौरी शिव शंकर प्यारी ॥

প্রলয়কাল সব নাশন হারী ।

তুম গৌরী শিব শংকর প্যারী ।।

pralayakāla saba nāśana hārī
tuma gaurī śiva śaṃkara pyārī

At the time of total dissolution you destroy all. You are the Goddess who is Rays of Light, beloved of Śiva, Śankar, the Cause of Peace.

शिव योगी तुम्हरे गुण गावें ।

ब्रह्मा विष्णु तुम्हें नित ध्यावें ॥

শিব যোগী তুম্হরে গুণ গাবেং ।

ব্রহ্মা বিষ্ণু তুম্হেং নিত ধ্যাবেং ।।

śiva yogī tumhare guṇa gāveṃ
brahmā viṣṇu tumheṃ nita dhyāveṃ

Śiva and all yogis sing of your qualities. Brahma and Viṣṇu always meditate upon you.

रूप सरस्वति का तुम धारा ।

दै सुबुद्धि ऋषि मुनिन उवारा ॥

রূপ সরস্বতি কা তুম ধারা ।

দৈ সুবুদ্ধি ঋষি মুনিন উবারা ।।

rūpa sarasvati kā tuma dhārā
dai subuddhi ṛṣi munina uvārā

You wear the form of Sarasvati, Goddess of Knowledge. You give excellent knowledge which liberates the ṛṣis and munis.

धर्‌यो रूप नरसिंह को अम्बा ।

प्रकट भईं विदारि कै खम्बा ॥

ধর্‌য়ো রূপ নরসিংহ কো অম্বা ।

প্রকট ভঈং বিদারি কৈ খম্বা ॥

dharyo rūpa narasiṃha ko ambā
prakaṭa bhaīṃ vidāri kai khambā
You gave the form for Narasingha to wear, Mother, which manifested with the crumbling of the pillar.

रक्षा करि प्रहलाद बचायो ।

हिरण्यकशिपु को स्वर्ग पठायो ॥

রক্ষা করি প্রহলাদ বচায়ো ।

হিরণ্যকশিপু কো স্বর্গ পঠায়ো ॥

rakṣā kari prahalāda bacāyo
hiraṇyakaśipu ko svarga paṭhāyo
Oh Protector, you saved Prahalad, and sent Hiraṇyakaśipu to heaven.

लक्ष्मी रूप धर्‌यो जगमाँही ।

श्री नारायण अङ्ग समाहीं ॥

লক্ষ্মী রূপ ধর্‌য়ো জগমাঁহী ।

শ্রী নারায়ণ অঙ্গ সমাহীং ॥

lakṣmī rūpa dharyo jagamām̐hī
śrī nārāyaṇa aṅga samāhīṃ
You wear the form of Lakṣmi, Oh Mother of the Universe, which is regarded the same as the body of the Respected Nārāyaṇa.

क्षीरसिन्धु में करत बिलासा।
दयासिन्धु दीजै मन आसा॥
ক্ষীরসিন্ধু মেং করত বিলাসা ।
দয়াসিন্ধু দীজৈ মন আসা ।।

kṣīrasindhu meṃ karata bilāsā
dayāsindhu dījai mana āsā

You are delighted in the ocean of milk. Oh Ocean of Compassion, please grant the mind's wish.

हिंगुलाज में तुम्ही भवानी।
महिमा अमित न जात बखानी॥
হিংগুলাজ মেং তুম্হী ভবানী ।
মহিমা অমিত ন জাত বখানী ।।

hiṃgulāja meṃ tumhī bhavānī
mahimā amita na jāta bakhānī

In the Hiṅgulaj you are Bhavānī, the Mother of Existence. No one who is born can describe your greatness.

मातंगी धूमावति माता।
भुवनेश्वरि बंगला सुखदाता॥
মাতঙ্গী ধূমাবতি মাতা ।
ভুবনেশ্বরি বঙ্গলা সুখদাতা ।।

mātaṃgī dhūmāvati mātā
bhuvaneśvari baṃgalā sukhadātā

You are Mātaṅgī and Mother Dhūmāvati. As Bhuvaneśvari and Baṃgala you grant comfort and happiness.

श्री भैरवी जगत की तारिणी ।

छिन्न भाल भव दुःख निवारिणी ॥

শ্রী ভৈরবী জগত কী তারিণী ।

ছিন্ন ভাল ভব দুঃখ নিবারিণী ।।

śrī bhairavī jagata kī tāriṇī
chinna bhāla bhava duḥkha nivāriṇī

As the respected fearful Bhairavī you deliver all the worlds. As Chinnamaṣṭa you prohibit pain in all the worlds.

लाँगुर बीर करत अगबानी ।

केहरि बाहन सोह भवानी ॥

লাঁগুর বীর করত অগবানী ।

কেহরি বাহন সোহ ভবানী ।।

lāṁgura bīra karata agabānī
kehari bāhana soha bhavānī

The excellent among the monkeys went to welcome you, oh Bhavānī, you who ride upon the lion.

कर महे खप्पर खड्ग विराजे ।

जाहि विलोकि काल भय भाजे ॥

কর মহে খপ্পর খড়্গ বিরাজে ।

জাহি বিলোকি কাল ভয় ভাজে ।।

kara mahe khappara khaṅga virāje
jāhi viloki kāla bhaya bhāje

In your hands are the sword and a beggar's bowl. The Seer experiences the fear of Time, the Great Destroyer.

कर शोभित तब मातु त्रिशूला ।

जाते उठत शत्रु हिय शूला ॥

কর শোভিত তব মাতু ত্রিশূলা ।

জাতে উঠত শত্রু হিয় শূলা ।।

kara śobhita taba mātu triśūlā
jāte uṭhata śatru hiya śūlā

Then in Mother's hand is seen the trident by which She abolishes the enemy's spear.

नगरकोट में तुम्हीं विराजत ।

तिंहूँ लोक में डंका वाजत ॥

নগরকোট মেং তুম্হীং বিরাজত ।

তিংহূঁ লোক মেং ডংকা বাজত ।।

nagarakoṭa meṃ tumhīṃ virājata
tiṃhūṁ loka meṃ ḍaṃkā vājata

In Nagarkoṭ you are known as Virāja, and the people of the three worlds beat on drums to celebrate you.

शुंभ निशुंभ दैत्य तुम मारे ।

रक्तबीज अगनित संहारे ॥

শুম্ভ নিশুম্ভ দৈত্য তুম মারে ।

রক্তবীজ অগনিত সংহারে ।।

śuṃbha niśuṃbha daitya tuma māre
raktabīja aganita saṃhāre

You slayed the demons Self-Conceit and Self-Deprecation. You dissolved the innumerable Seeds of Desire.

महिषासुर नृप अति अभिमानी ।

जेहि अघ भार मही अकुलानी ॥

মহিষাসুর নৃপ অতি অভিমানী ।

জেহি অঘ ভার মহী অকুলানী ।।

mahiṣāsura nṛpa ati abhimānī
jehi agha bhāra mahī akulānī

The King Great Ego was extremely proud. The burden of his guilt for sins brought him down low.

रूप कराल कालिका धारा ।

सैन्य सहित तुम ताहि सँहारा ॥

রূপ করাল কালিকা ধারা ।

সৈন্য সহিত তুম তাহি সঁহারা ।।

rūpa karāla kālikā dhārā
sainya sahita tuma tāhi saṁhārā

As Kālī you wear an immense form. You destroyed the entire army in battle.

परी भीर सन्तन पै जब जब ।

भईं सहाय मातु तुम तब तब ॥

পরী ভীর সন্তন পৈ জব জব ।

ভঈং সহায় মাতু তুম তব তব ।।

parī bhīra santana pai jaba jaba
bhaīṃ sahāya mātu tuma taba taba

Whenever your children are burdened with perplexity, then and there you manifest, Oh Mother, to render assistance.

अमरपुरी अरु बासव लोका ।

तब महिमा सब रहहि अशोका ॥

অমরপুরী অরু বাসব লোকা ।

তব মহিমা সব রহহি অশোকা ।।

amarapurī aru bāsava lokā
taba mahimā saba rahahi aśokā

Again and again you lead people to dwell in immortality. Then all elucidate your greatness with great joy and tranquility.

वाला में है ज्योति तुम्हारी ।

पूजहिं तुमहिं सदा नर नारी ॥

বালা মেং হৈ জ্যোতি তুম্হারী ।

পূজহিং তুমহিং সদা নর নারী ।।

vālā meṃ hai jyoti tumhārī
pūjahiṃ tumahiṃ sadā nara nārī

In all the inhabitants your light is burning. Men and women always perform your worship.

प्रेम भक्तियुत जो यश गावहिं ।

दुख दारिद्र निकट नहिं आवहिं ॥

প্রেম ভক্তিয়ুত জো যশ গাবহিং ।

দুখ দারিদ্র নিকট নহিং আবহিং ।।

prema bhaktiyuta jo yaśa gāvahiṃ
dukha dāridra nikaṭa nahiṃ āvahiṃ

Whoever will sing this praise with love and devotion, pain and discomfort will not come close to them.

ध्यावहिं तुम्हें जो नर मनलाई ।

जान्म मरण ते सो छुटि जाई ॥

ধ্যাবহিং তুম্হেং জো নর মনলাঈ ।

জান্ম মরণ তে সো ছুটি জাঈ ।।

dhyāvahiṃ tumheṃ jo nara manalāī
jānma maraṇa te so chuṭi jāī

Whoever will meditate on you with full concentration, will escape from the cycle of birth and death.

जोगी सुर मुनि कहत पुकारी ।

योग न हो बिनु शक्ति तुम्हारी ॥

যোগী সুর মুনি কহত পুকারী ।

যোগ ন হো বিনু শক্তি তুম্হারী ।।

jogī sura muni kahata pukārī
yoga na ho binu śakti tumhārī

The yogis, Gods, and munis all call out, "Without your energy union is impossible!"

शिवशंकर अचरज तप कीन्हा ।

काम क्रोध कहैं बस करि लीन्हा ॥

শিবশংকর অচরজ তপ কীন্হা ।

কাম ক্রোধ কহৈং বস করি লীন্হা ।।

śivaśaṃkara acaraja tapa kīnhā
kāma krodha kahaiṃ basa kari līnhā

Śiva Śankar performed a most wonderful tapasya by which He defeated Anger and Passion.

निशिदिन ध्यान धरहु शंकर को ।

काहु काल नहिं सुमिरो तुमको ॥

নিশিদিন ধ্যান ধরহু শংকর কো ।

কাহু কাল নহিং সুমিরো তুমকো ।।

niśidina dhyāna dharahu śaṃkara ko
kāhu kāla nahiṃ sumiro tumako

Even though one meditates upon Śiva every day, he can never reach to the heights of your attainment.

शक्ति रूप को मरम न पायो ।

शक्ति गई तब मन पछितायो ॥

শক্তি রূপ কো মরম ন পায়ো ।

শক্তি গঈ তব মন পছিতায়ো ।।

śakti rūpa ko marama na pāyo
śakti gaī taba mana pachitāyo

The form of energy is never destroyed. Who sings in praise of Energy, his mind will endure.

शरणागत हुई कीर्ति बखानी ।

जय जय जय जगदम्ब भवानी ॥

শরণাগত হুঈ কীর্তি বখানী ।

জয় জয় জয় জগদম্ব ভবানী ।।

śaraṇāgata huī kīrti bakhānī
jaya jaya jaya jagadamba bhavānī

Who takes refuge in you, fame will increase. Victory, victory, victory to the Divine Mother of the Universe, Mother of Existence!

भईं प्रसन्न आदि जगदम्बा ।

दीन्ह शक्ति नहिं कीन्ह विलम्बा ॥

ভঈং প্রসন্ন আদি জগদম্বা ।

দীন্হ শক্তি নহিং কীন্হ বিলম্বা ।।

bhaīṃ prasanna ādi jagadambā
dīnha śakti nahiṃ kīnha vilambā

Please be pleased, Oh Mother of the Universe. Give me energy without further delay.

मोको मातु कष्ट अति घेरो ।

तुम बिनु कौन हरे दुःख मेरो ॥

মোকো মাতু কষ্ট অতি ঘেরো ।

তুম বিনু কৌন হরে দুঃখ মেরো ।।

moko mātu kaṣṭa ati ghero
tuma binu kauna hare duḥkha mero

Oh Mother, I am surrounded by difficulties. Other than you, who can take away my pain?

आशा तृषणा निपट सतावै ।

रिपु मूरख मोहि अति डरपावै ॥

আশা তৃষণা নিপট সতাবৈ ।

রিপু মূরখ মোহি অতি ডরপাবৈ ।।

āśā tṛṣṇā nipaṭa satāvai
ripu mūrakha mohi ati ḍarapāvai

Wishes and desires are extremely tormenting. The ignorance caused by foolish limitations is extremely fearful.

दुर्गा पूजा Durgā Pūjā

शत्रु नाश कीजै महारानी ।
सुमिराहु एक चित तुमहि भवानी ॥

শত্রু নাশ কীজৈ মহারানী ।
সুমিরাহু এক চিত তুমহি ভবানী ।।

śatru nāśa kījai mahārānī
sumirāhu eka cita tumahi bhavānī

Oh Great Queen, please destroy all enemies. Let me recollect One Consciousness, and let that be You, Oh Mother of Existence.

करहु कृपा हे मातु दयाला ।
ऋद्धि सिद्धि दै करहु निहाला ॥

করহু কৃপা হে মাতু দয়ালা ।
ঋদ্ধি সিদ্ধি দৈ করহু নিহালা ।।

karahu kṛpā he mātu dayālā
ṛddhi siddhi dai karahu nihālā

Give me your Grace, Oh Compassionate Mother. Give increase to perfection causing Supreme Happiness.

जब लगि जियहुँ दया फल पाऊँ ।
तुम्हारो जस मैं सदा सुनाऊँ ॥

জব লগি জিয়হুঁ দয়া ফল পাউঁ ।
তুম্হারো জস মৈং সদা সুনাউঁ ।।

jaba lagi jiyahuṁ dayā phala pāūṁ
tumhāro jasa maiṃ sadā sunāūṁ

When the fruit of Compassion touches my heart, I only want to always sing your praises.

दुर्गा चालीसा जो नर गावैं ।

सब सुख भोगि परम पद पावैं ॥

দুর্গা চালীসা জো নর গাবৈং ।

সব সুখ ভোগি পরম পদ পাবৈং ।।

durgā cālīsā jo nara gāvaiṃ
saba sukha bhogi parama pada pāvaiṃ

Whoever sings this Durgā Cālīsā, Praise of the Divine Mother, will enjoy the highest happiness and attain the most exalted respect.

मो कहँ निज शरणागत जानी ।

करहु कृपा जगदम्ब भवानी ॥

মো কহঁ নিজ শরণাগত জানী ।

করহু কৃপা জগদম্ব ভবানী ।।

mo kahaṁ nija śaraṇāgata jānī
karahu kṛpā jagadamba bhavānī

Where will I find my own refuge? Please give me your Grace, Oh Mother of the Universe, Mother of Existence.

दोहा

দোহা

dohā

सिंहावाहिनी मातु तुम मुदमंगल दातार ।

करहु कृपा जनि जानिके पर्‌यो तुम्हारे द्वार ॥

সিংহাবাহিনী মাতু তুম মুদমঙ্গল দাতার ।

করহু কৃপা জনি জানিকে পর্য্যো তুম্হারে দ্বার ।।

siṃhāvāhinī mātu tuma mudamaṃgala dātāra
karahu kṛpā jani jānike paryo tumhāre dvāra

दुर्गा पूजा Durgā Pūjā

Mother, you ride upon a lion, Grantor of Delight and Welfare. Oh Mother of all beings, give Grace to your children, who have fallen at your door.

श्री दुर्गा माता कि जय

শ্রী দুর্গা মাতা কি জয়

śrī durgā mātā ki jaya
Victory to the respected Durgā Mā

चण्डी माँ की आरती

চণ্ডী মাঁ কী আরতী

caṇḍī mā kī āratī
Be Victorious!

जय चण्डी जय जय (माँ) जय चण्डी जय जय

भयहारिणि भवतारिणि भवभामिनि जय जय

ॐ जय चण्डी जय जय

জয় চণ্ডী জয় জয় (মাঁ) জয় চণ্ডী জয় জয়

ভয়হারিণি ভবতারিণি ভবভামিনি জয় জয়

জয় চণ্ডী জয় জয়

jaya caṇḍī jaya jaya (māṁ) jaya caṇḍī jaya jaya
bhaya hāriṇi bhava tāriṇi (2) bhava bhāmini jaya jaya
oṃ jaya caṇḍī jaya jaya
Be Victorious! Oh Goddess Who Tears Apart Thought! Be Victorious! You take away all fear and illuminate the intensity of reality. Be Victorious!

दुर्गा पूजा Durgā Pūjā

तू ही सत-चित-सुखमय शुद्ध ब्रह्मरूपा (माँ)

सत्य सनातन सुन्दर पर-शिव सूर-भूपा

ॐ जय चण्डी जय जय

তূ হী সত-চিত-সুখময় শূদ্ধ ব্রহ্মরূপা (মাঁ)

সত্য সনাতন সুন্দর পর-শিব সূর-ভূপা

জয় চণ্ডী জয় জয়

tū hī sata cita sukhamaya śuddha brahmarūpā (māṁ)
satya sanātana sundara (2) para śiva sūra bhūpā
oṃ jaya caṇḍī jaya jaya

You are the essence of Truth, Consciousness, Happiness, the form of Pure Conscious Being. You are the beauty of Eternal Truth. Beyond infinite goodness, you rule over all the Gods. Be Victorious!

आदि अनादि अनामय अविचल अविनाशी (माँ)

अमल अनन्त अगोचर अज आनन्दराशी

ॐ जय चण्डी जय जय

আদি অনাদি অনাময় অবিচল অবিনাশী (মাঁ)

অমল অনন্ত অগোচর অজ আনন্দরাশী

জয় চণ্ডী জয় জয়

ādi anādi anāmaya avicala avināśī (māṁ)
amala ananta agocara (2) aja ānandarāśī
oṃ jaya caṇḍī jaya jaya

The beginning, without beginning, unseverable; motionless and indestructible; Bright, infinite, imperceptible, unborn, the great collection of Bliss. Be Victorious!

दुर्गा पूजा Durgā Pūjā

अविकारी अघहारी अकल कलाधारी (माँ)

कर्त्ता विधि भर्त्ता हरि हर सँहारकारी

ॐ जय चण्डी जय जय

অবিকারী অঘহারী অকল কলাধারী (মাঁ)

কর্ত্তা বিধি ভর্ত্তা হরি হর সঁহারকারী

জয় চণ্ডী জয় জয়

avikārī aghahārī akala kalādhārī (mām̐)
karttā vidhi bharttā hari (2) hara sam̐hārakārī
oṃ jaya caṇḍī jaya jaya
Changeless, holy One, sinless, bearer of individual phenomena; created by Brahmā, sustained by Viṣṇu, and Śiva who dissolves this creation. Be Victorious!

तू विधि वधू रमा तू उमा महामाया (माँ)

मूलप्रकृति विद्या तू तू जननी जाया

ॐ जय चण्डी जय जय

তূ বিধি বধূ রমা তূ উমা মহামায়া (মাঁ)

মূলপ্রকৃতি বিদ্যা তূ তূ জননী জায়া

জয় চণ্ডী জয় জয়

tū vidhi vadhū ramā tū umā mahā māyā (mām̐)
mūlaprakṛti vidyā tū (2) tū jananī jāyā
oṃ jaya caṇḍī jaya jaya
You are the wife of Brahmā, the wife of Viṣṇu (Ramā), the wife of Śiva (Umā), the Great Measurement of Conscious-ness. You are the knowledge of primordial existence, the Mother who gives birth to all. Be Victorious!

राम कृष्ण तू सीता ब्रजरानी राधा (माँ)

तू वाञ्छाकल्पद्रुम हारिणि सब बाधा

ॐ जय चण्डी जय जय

রাম কৃষ্ণ তূ সীতা ব্রজরানী রাধা (মাঁ)

তূ বাঞ্ছাকল্পদ্রুম হারিণি সব বাধা

জয় চণ্ডী জয় জয়

rāma kṛṣṇa tū sītā brajarānī rādhā (māṁ)
tū vāñchā kalpadruma (2) hāriṇi saba bādhā
oṃ jaya caṇḍī jaya jaya

You are the consciousness of the subtle light of wisdom which merges with the ultimate. You are the Doer of All. You are Sītā, the pure white one, the Queen of the multitude; Rādhā, the Ruler of all success. You are the desire of the wishfulfilling tree, taking away all obstructions. Be Victorious!

दश विद्या नव दुर्गा नानाशस्त्रकरा (माँ)

अष्टमातृका योगिनि नव नव रूप धरा

ॐ जय चण्डी जय जय

দশ বিদ্যা নব দূর্গা নানাশস্ত্রকরা (মাঁ)

অষ্টমাতৃকা যোগিনি নব নব রূপ ধরা

জয় চণ্ডী জয় জয়

daśa vidyā nava durgā nānāśastra karā (māṁ)
aṣṭa mātṛkā yogini (2) nava nava rūpa dharā
oṃ jaya caṇḍī jaya jaya

You are the ten branches of knowledge (Mahā Vidyās), nine Relievers of Difficulties (nine Durgās). The various scriptures present you. The eight Mothers of union. Various are the forms that you assume. Be Victorious!

तू परधामनिवासिनि महाविलासिनि तू (माँ)

तू ही श्मशानविहारिणि ताण्डवलासिनि तू

ॐ जय चण्डी जय जय

তূ পরধামনিবাসিনি মহাবিলাসিনি তূ (মাঁ)

তূ হী শ্মশানবিহারিণি তাণ্ডবলাসিনি তূ

জয় চণ্ডী জয় জয়

tū paradhāma nivāsini mahā vilāsini tū (mām̐)
tū hī śmaśāna vihāriṇi (2) tāṇḍavalāsini tū
oṃ jaya caṇḍī jaya jaya

You are the inhabitant of the highest residence. Yours is the greatest beauty. You wander about the cremation grounds dancing to the rhythmic music. Be Victorious!

सुर मुनि मोहिनि सौम्या तू शोभाऽऽधारा (माँ)

विवसनविकट-सरूपा प्रलयमयी धारा

ॐ जय चण्डी जय जय

সুর মুনি মোহিনি সৌম্যা তূ শোভাঽঽধারা (মাঁ)

বিবসনবিকট-সরূপা প্রলয়ময়ী ধারা

জয় চণ্ডী জয় জয়

sura muni mohini saumyā tū śobhā--dhārā (mām̐)
vivasana vikaṭ sarūpā (2) pralaya mayī dhārā
oṃ jaya caṇḍī jaya jaya

You mesmerize the Gods and munis when you present your radiant beauty. All are helpless seeing your dreadful appearance at the time when you assume the form of total dissolution. Be Victorious!

तू ही स्नेह-सुधामयि तू अति गरलमना (माँ)

रत्नविभूषित तू ही तू ही अस्थि तना

ॐ जय चण्डी जय जय

তূ হী স্নেহ-সুধাময়ি তূ অতি গরলমনা (মাঁ)

রত্নবিভূষিত তূ হী তূ হী অস্থি তনা

জয় চণ্ডী জয় জয়

tū hī sneha sudhāmayi tū ati garalamanā (mām̐)
ratna vibhūṣita tū hī (2) tū hī asthi tanā
oṃ jaya caṇḍī jaya jaya

You pervade Love and ease. You are extremely eminent. You are the Brilliance of the jewel. You are the invisible existence. Be Victorious!

मूलाधारनिवासिनि इह पर सिद्धि प्रदे (माँ)

कालातीता काली कमल तू वरदे

ॐ जय चण्डी जय जय

মূলাধারনিবাসিনি ইহ পর সিদ্ধি প্রদে (মাঁ)

কালাতীতা কালী কমল তূ বরদে

জয় চণ্ডী জয় জয়

mūlādhāra nivāsini iha para siddhi prade (mām̐)
kālātītā kālī (2) kamala tū varade
oṃ jaya caṇḍī jaya jaya

You reside in the Mūlādhāra Chakra. You grant the highest attainment in this world. At the appointed time you are Kālī, the Remover of Darkness, and as the Lotus One you grant blessings. Be Victorious!

दुर्गा पूजा Durgā Pūjā

शक्ति शक्तिधर तू ही नित्य अभेदमयी (माँ)

भेदप्रदर्शिनि वाणी विमले वेदत्रयी

ॐ जय चण्डी जय जय

শক্তি শক্তিধর তূ হী নিত্য অভেদময়ী (মাঁ)

ভেদপ্রদর্শিনি বাণী বিমলে বেদত্রয়ী

জয় চণ্ডী জয় জয়

śakti śakti dhara tū hī nitya abheda mayī (mām̐)
bheda pradarśini vāṇī (2) vimale vedatrayī
oṃ jaya caṇḍī jaya jaya

You are every form of energy, the eternal undistinguishable essence, the vibration which exposes change and distinction, and the spotlessly pure three Vedas. Be Victorious!

हम अति दीन दुखी माँ विपत-जाल घेरे (माँ)

हैं कपूत अति कपटी पर बालक तेरे

ॐ जय चण्डी जय जय

হম অতি দীন দুখী মাঁ বিপত-জাল ঘেরে (মাঁ)

হৈং কপূত অতি কপটী পর বালক তেরে

জয় চণ্ডী জয় জয়

ham ati dīna dukhī mām̐ vipat jāla ghere (mām̐)
haiṃ kapūt ati kapaṭī (2) para bālaka tere
oṃ jaya caṇḍī jaya jaya

Since so many days we are in pain, Maa. We are bound by adversities and suffering. We are negligent and insincere, but still we are your children. Be Victorious!

दुर्गा पूजा Durgā Pūjā

निज स्वभाववश जननी दया दृष्टि कीजै (माँ)

करुणा कर करुणामयि चरण-शरण दीजै

ॐ जय चण्डी जय जय

নিজ স্বভাববশ জননী দয়া দৃষ্ট্রি কীজৈ (মাঁ)

করুণা কর করুণাময়ি চরণ-শরণ দীজৈ

জয় চণ্ডী জয় জয়

nija svabhāva vaśa jananī dayā dṛṣṭi kījai (māṁ)
karuṇā kara karuṇā mayi (2) caraṇa śaraṇa dījai
oṃ jaya caṇḍī jaya jaya

Endow us with your very own nature, Mother. Give us your mercy, Oh Merciful Mother! Give us the refuge of your lotus feet. Be Victorious!

जय चण्डी जय जय (माँ) जय चण्डी जय जय

भयहारिणि भवतारिणि भवभामिनि जय जय

ॐ जय चण्डी जय जय

জয় চণ্ডী জয় জয় (মাঁ) জয় চণ্ডী জয় জয়

ভয়হারিণি ভবতারিণি ভবভামিনি জয় জয়

জয় চণ্ডী জয় জয়

jaya caṇḍī jaya jaya (māṁ) jaya caṇḍī jaya jaya
bhaya hāriṇi bhava tāriṇi (2) bhava bhāmini jaya jaya
oṃ jaya caṇḍī jaya jaya

Be Victorious! Oh Goddess Who Tears Apart Thought! Be Victorious! You take away all fear and illuminate the intensity of reality. Be Victorious!

Closing Prayers

दुर्गां शिवां शान्तिकरीं ब्रह्माणीं ब्रह्मणः प्रियाम् ।
सर्वलोक प्रणेत्रीञ्च प्रणमामि सदा शिवाम् ॥

দূর্গাং শিবাং শান্তিকরীং ব্রহ্মাণীং ব্রহ্মণঃ প্রিয়াম্ ।
সর্বলোক প্রণেত্রীঞ্চ প্রণমামি সদা শিবাম্ ।।

durgāṃ śivāṃ śāntikarīṃ brahmāṇīṃ brahmaṇaḥ priyām
sarvaloka praṇetrīñca praṇamāmi sadā śivām

The Reliever of Difficulties, Exposer of Goodness, Cause of Peace, Infinite Consciousness, Beloved by Knowers of Consciousness; all the inhabitants of all the worlds always bow to Her, and I am bowing to Goodness Herself.

मङ्गलां शोभनां शुद्धां निष्कलां परमां कलाम् ।
विश्वेश्वरीं विश्वमातां चण्डिकां प्रणमाम्यहम् ॥

মঙ্গলাং শোভনাং শুদ্ধাং নিষ্কলাং পরমাং কলাম্ ।
বিশ্বেশ্বরীং বিশ্বমাতাং চণ্ডিকাং প্রণমাম্যহম্ ।।

maṅgalāṃ śobhanāṃ śuddhāṃ niṣkalāṃ paramāṃ kalām
viśveśvarīṃ viśvamātāṃ caṇḍikāṃ praṇamāmyaham

Welfare, Radiant Beauty, Completely Pure, Without Limitations, the Ultimate Limitation, the Lord of the Universe, the Mother of the Universe, to you Caṇḍi, to the Energy which Tears Apart Thought, I bow in submission.

सर्वदेवमयीं देवीं सर्वरोगभयापहाम् ।
ब्रह्मेशविष्णुनमितां प्रणमामि सदा शिवाम् ॥

সর্বদেবময়ীং দেবীং সর্বরোগভয়াপহাম্ ।
ব্রহ্মেশবিষ্ণুনমিতাং প্রণমামি সদা শিবাম্ ।।

sarvadevamayīṃ devīṃ sarvarogabhayāpahām
brahmeśaviṣṇunamitāṃ praṇamāmi sadā śivām

Composed of all the Gods, removing all sickness and fear, Brahma, Maheshwar and Viṣṇu bow down to Her, and I always bow down to the Energy of Infinite Goodness.

विन्ध्यस्थां विन्ध्यनिलयां दिव्यस्थाननिवासिनीम् ।

योगिनीं योगजननीं चण्डिकां प्रणमाम्यहम् ॥

বিন্ধ্যস্থাং বিন্ধ্যনিলয়াং দিব্যস্থাননিবাসিনীম্ ।

যোগিনীং যোগজননীং চণ্ডিকাং প্রণমাম্যহম্ ।।

vindhyasthāṃ vindhyanilayāṃ divyasthānanivāsinīm
yoginīṃ yogajananīṃ caṅḍikāṃ praṇamāmyaham

The dwelling place of Knowledge, residing in Knowledge, Resident in the place of Divine Illumination, the Cause of Union, the Knower of Union, to the Energy Which Tears Apart Thought we constantly bow.

ईशानमातरं देवीमीश्वरीमीश्वरप्रियाम् ।

प्रणतोऽस्मि सदा दुर्गां संसारार्णवतारिणीम् ॥

ঈশানমাতরং দেবীমীশ্বরীমীশ্বরপ্রিয়াম্ ।

প্রণতোঽস্মি সদা দুর্গাং সংসারার্ণবতারিণীম্ ।।

Īśānamātaraṃ devīmīśvarīmīśvarapriyām
praṇato-smi sadā durgāṃ saṃsārārṇavatāriṇīm

The Mother of the Supreme Consciousness, the Goddess Who is the Supreme Consciousness, beloved by the Supreme Consciousness, we always bow to Durgā, the Reliever of Difficulties, who takes aspirants across the difficult sea of objects and their relationships.

दुर्गा पूजा Durgā Pūjā

ॐ महादेव महात्रान महायोगि महेश्वर ।

सर्वपाप हरां देव मकाराय नमो नमः ॥

ওঁ মহাদেব মহাত্রান মহাযোগি মহেশ্বর ।

সর্বপাপ হরাং দেব মকারায় নমো নমঃ ।।

oṃ mahādeva mahātrāna mahāyogi maheśvara
sarvapāpa harāṃ deva makārāya namo namaḥ

Oṃ The Great God, the Great Reliever, the Great Yogi, Oh Supreme Lord, Oh God who removes all Sin, in the form of the letter "M" which dissolves creation, we bow to you again and again.

ॐ नमः शिवाय शान्ताय कारणत्राय हेतवे ।

निवेदायामि चात्मानं त्वं गति परमेश्वर ॥

ওঁ নমঃ শিবায় শান্তায় কারণত্রায় হেতবে ।

নিবেদায়ামি চাত্মানং ত্বং গতি পরমেশ্বর ।।

oṃ namaḥ śivāya śāntāya kāraṇatrāya hetave
nivedāyāmi cātmānaṃ tvaṃ gati parameśvara

Oṃ I bow to the Consciousness of Infinite Goodness, to Peace, to the Cause of the three worlds, I offer to you the fullness of my soul, Oh Supreme Lord.

त्वमेव माता च पिता त्वमेव त्वमेव बन्धुश्च सखा त्वमेव ।

त्वमेव विद्या द्रविनं त्वमेव त्वमेव सर्वम् मम देवदेव ॥

ত্বমেব মাতা চ পিতা ত্বমেব ত্বমেব বন্ধুশ্চ সখা ত্বমেব ।

ত্বমেব বিদ্যা দ্রবিনং ত্বমেব ত্বমেব সর্বম্ মম দেবদেব ।।

tvameva mātā ca pitā tvameva
tvameva bandhuśca sakhā tvameva
tvameva vidyā dravinaṃ tvameva
tvameva sarvam mama deva deva

You alone are Mother and Father, you alone are friend and relative. You alone are knowledge and wealth, Oh my God of Gods, you alone are everything.

कयेन वच मनसेन्द्रियैर्व बुद्ध्यात्मा नव प्रकृत स्वभवत् ।
करोमि यद्यत् सकलम् परस्मै नारायणायेति समर्पयामि ॥

কয়েন বচ মনসেন্দ্রিয়ৈর্ব বুদ্ধ্যাত্মা নব প্রকৃত স্বভবৎ ।
করোমি যদ্যৎ সকলম্ পরস্মৈ নারায়ণায়েতি সমর্পয়ামি ।।

kayena vaca manasendriyairva
buddhyātmā nava prakṛta svabhavat
karomi yadyat sakalam parasmai
nārāyaṇāyeti samarpayāmi

Body, speech, mind, the five organs of knowledge (five senses) and the intellect; these nine are the natural condition of human existence. In their highest evolution, I move beyond them all, as I surrender completely to the Supreme Consciousness.

ॐ पापोऽहं पापकर्महं पापात्मा पापसम्भव ।
त्राहिमं पुण्डरीकक्षं सर्वपाप हरो हरि ॥

ওঁ পাপোঽহং পাপকর্মহং পাপাত্মা পাপসম্ভব ।
ত্রাহিমং পুণ্ডরীকক্ষং সর্বপাপ হরো হরি ।।

oṃ pāpo-haṃ pāpakarmahaṃ pāpātmā pāpasambhava
trāhimaṃ puṇḍarīkakṣaṃ sarvapāpa haro hari

Oṃ I am of sin, confusion, duality; my actions are of duality; this entire existence is of duality. Oh Savior and Protector, Oh Great Consciousness, take away all sin, confusion, duality.

ॐ मन्त्रहीनं क्रियाहीनं भक्तिहीनं सुरेश्वरि ।
यत्पूजितं मया देवि परिपूर्णं तदस्तु मे ॥

ওঁ মন্ত্রহীনং ক্রিয়াহীনং ভক্তিহীনং সুরেশ্বরি ।
যৎপূজিতং ময়া দেবি পরিপূর্ণং তদস্তু মে ।।

oṃ mantrahīnaṃ kriyāhīnaṃ bhaktihīnaṃ sureśvari
yatpūjitaṃ mayā devi paripūrnaṃ tadastu me

Oṃ I know nothing of mantras. I do not perform good conduct. I have no devotion, Oh Supreme Goddess. But Oh my Goddess, please accept the worship that I offer.

त्वमेव प्रत्यक्षम् ब्रह्माऽसि । त्वमेव प्रत्यक्षम् ब्रह्मा वदिश्यामि ।
रितम् वदिश्यामि, सत्यम् वदिश्यामि । तन मामवतु,
तद वक्तारमवतु । अवतु माम्, अवतु वक्तारम् ॥

ত্বমেব প্রত্যক্ষম্ ব্রহ্মাঽসি । ত্বমেব প্রত্যক্ষম্ ব্রহ্মা বদিশ্যামি।
রিতম্ বদিশ্যামি, সত্যম্ বদিশ্যামি ।
তন মামবতু, তদ বক্তারমবতু ।
অবতু মাম্, অবতু বক্তারম্ ।।

tvameva pratyakṣam brahmā-si tvameva pratyakṣam brahmā vadiśyāmi ritam vadiśyāmi, satyam vadiśyāmi tan māmavatu, tad vaktāramavatu avatu mām, avatu vaktāram

You alone are the Perceivable Supreme Divinity. You alone are the Perceivable Supreme Divinity, so I shall declare. I shall speak the nectar of immortality. I shall speak Truth. May this body be your instrument. May this mouth be your instrument. May the Divine always be with us. May it be thus.

ॐ सह नाववतु, सह नौ भुनक्तु । सह वीर्यं करवावहै ।
तेजस्विनावधीतमस्तु । मा विद्विशावहै ॥

ওঁ সহ নাববতু, সহ নৌ ভুনক্তু ।
সহ বীর্যং করবাবহৈ । তেজস্বিনাবধীতমস্তু ।
মা বিদ্বিশাবহৈ ।।

oṃ saha nāvavatu saha nau bhunaktu
saha vīryam karavāvahai
tejasvināvadhītamastu mā vidviśāvahai

Oṃ May the Lord protect us. May the Lord grant us enjoyment of all actions. May we be granted strength to work together. May our studies be thorough and faithful. May all disagreement cease.

ॐ असतो मा सद्गमय । तमसो मा ज्योतिर्गमय ।

मृत्योर्मा अमृतं गमय ॥

ওঁ অসতো মা সদ্গময় । তমসো মা জ্যোতির্গময় ।

মৃত্যোর্মা অমৃতং গময় ।।

oṃ asatomā sadgamaya
tamasomā jyotirgamaya
mṛtyormā amṛtaṃ gamaya

Oṃ From the untruth lead us to Truth. From darkness lead us to the Light. From death lead us to Immortality.

ॐ सर्वेषं स्वस्तिर्भवतु । सर्वेषं शान्तिर्भवतु । सर्वेषं पूर्णं भवतु ।

सर्वेषं मङ्गलं भवतु । सर्वे भवन्तु सुखिनः । सर्वे शन्तु निरमयाः ।

सर्वे भद्राणि पश्यन्तु । मा कश्चिद् दुःख भाग्भवेत् ॥

ওঁ সর্বেষং স্বস্তির্ভবতু । সর্বেষং শান্তির্ভবতু । সর্বেষং

পূর্ণং ভবতু । সর্বেষং মঙ্গলং ভবতু । সর্বে ভবন্তু

সুখিনঃ । সর্বে শন্তু নিরময়াঃ । সর্বে ভদ্রাণি পশ্যন্তু ।

মা কশ্চিদ্ দুঃখ ভাগ্ভবেৎ ।।

oṃ sarveṣaṃ svastir bhavatu sarveṣaṃ śāntir bhavatu
sarveṣaṃ pūrṇaṃ bhavatu sarveṣaṃ maṅgalaṃ bhavatu
sarve bhavantu sukhinaḥ sarve śantu niramayāḥ
sarve bhadrāṇi paśyantu mā kaścid duḥkha bhāgbhavet

Oṃ May all be blessed with the highest realization. May all be blessed with Peace. May all be blessed with Perfection. May all be blessed with Welfare. May all be blessed with comfort and happiness. May all be free from misery. May all perceive auspiciousness. May all be free from infirmities.

गुरुर्ब्रह्मा गुरुर्विष्णुः गुरुर्देवो महेश्वरः ।
गुरुसाक्षात् परं ब्रह्मा तस्मै श्रीगुरवे नमः ॥

গুরুর্ব্রহ্মা গুরুর্বিষ্ণুঃ গুরুর্দেবো মহেশ্বরঃ ।
গুরুর্সাক্ষাৎ পরং ব্রহ্মা তস্মৈ শ্রীগুরবে নমঃ ।।

gurur brahmā gururviṣṇuḥ gururdevo maheśvaraḥ
gurusākṣāt paraṃ brahmā tasmai śrīgurave namaḥ

The Guru is Brahma, Guru is Viṣṇuḥ, Guru is the Lord Maheśvaraḥ. The Guru is actually the Supreme Divinity, and therefore we bow down to the Guru.

ॐ ब्रह्मार्पणं ब्रह्म हविर्ब्रह्माग्नौ ब्रह्मणा हुतम् ।
ब्रह्मैव तेन गन्तव्यं ब्रह्मकर्मसमाधिना ॥

ওঁ ব্রহ্মার্পণং ব্রহ্মা হবির্ব্রহ্মাগ্নৌ ব্রহ্মণা হুতম্ ।
ব্রহ্মৈব তেন গন্তব্যং ব্রহ্মকর্মসমাধিনা ।।

oṃ brahmārpaṇaṃ brahma havir
brahmāgnau brahmaṇā hutam
brahmaiva tena gantavyaṃ brahmakarmasamādhinā

Oṃ The Supreme Divinity makes the offering; the Supreme Divinity is the offering; offered by the Supreme Divinity, in the fire of the Supreme Divinity. By seeing the Supreme Divinity in all actions, one realizes that Supreme Divinity.

ॐ पूर्णमदः पूर्णमिदं पूर्णात् पूर्णमुदच्यते ।
पूर्णस्य पूर्णमादाय पूर्णमेवावशिश्यते ॥

ওঁ পূর্ণমদঃ পূর্ণমিদং পূর্ণাৎ পূর্ণমুদচ্যতে ।
পূর্ণস্য পূর্ণমাদায় পূর্ণমেবাবশিশ্যতে ।।

oṃ pūrṇamadaḥ pūrṇamidaṃ pūrṇāt pūrṇamudacyate
pūrṇasya pūrṇamādāya pūrṇamevāva śiṣyate

Oṃ That is whole and perfect; this is whole and perfect. From the whole and perfect, the whole and perfect becomes manifest. If the whole and perfect issue forth from the whole and perfect, even still only the whole and perfect will remain.

ॐ शान्तिः शान्तिः शान्तिः

ওঁ শান্তিঃ শান্তিঃ শান্তিঃ

oṃ śāntiḥ śāntiḥ śāntiḥ

Oṃ Peace, Peace, Peace

More Books by Shree Maa and Swami Satyananda Saraswati

Annapūrṇa Thousand Names
Before Becoming This
Bhagavad Gītā
Chaṇḍi Pāṭh
Cosmic Pūjā
Cosmic Pūjā Bengali
Devī Gītā
Devī Mandir Songbook
Durgā Pūjā Beginner
Ganeśa Pūjā
Gems From the Chaṇḍi
Guru Gītā
Hanumān Pūjā
Kālī Dhyānam
Kālī Pūjā
Lakṣmī Sahasra Nāma
Lalitā Triśati
Rudrāṣṭādhyāyī
Sahib Sadhu
Saraswati Pūjā for Children
Shree Maa's Favorite Recipes
Shree Maa - The Guru & the Goddess
Shree Maa, The Life of a Saint
Śiva Pūjā Beginner
Śiva Pūjā and Advanced Fire Ceremony
Sundara Kāṇḍa
Swāmī Purāṇa
Thousand Names of Ganeśa
Thousand Names of Gayatri
Thousand Names of Viṣṇu and
Satya Nārāyaṇa Vrata Kathā

CDs and Cassettes

Chaṇḍi Pāṭh
Durgā Pūjā Beginner
Lalitā Triśati
Mantras of the Nine Planets
Navarṇa Mantra
Oh Dark Night Mother
Oṃ Mantra
Sādhu Stories from the Himalayas
Shree Maa at the Devi Mandir
Shree Maa in the Temple of the Heart
Shiva is in My Heart
Shree Maa on Tour, 1998
Śiva Pūjā Beginner
Śiva Pūjā and Advanced Fire Ceremony
The Goddess is Everywhere
The Songs of Ramprasad
The Thousand Names of Kālī
Tryambakaṃ Mantra

Videos

Across the States with Shree Maa & Swamiji
Meaning and Method of Worship
Shree Maa: Meeting a Modern Saint
Visiting India with Shree Maa and Swamiji

Please visit us at www.shreemaa.org
Our email is info@shreemaa.or

CPSIA information can be obtained
at www.ICGtesting.com
Printed in the USA
FSHW010838070820
72683FS

9 781877 795305